MAKING A
DIFFERENCE

How a little upstart
eyewear company
changed the optical industry

By Al Berg
as told to
Frank Giammanco

TABLE OF CONTENTS

ON THE COVER: Marchon's mascots, the Fuzzies, became synonymous with the company and the red "O" in its first logo. Thousands were given out to customers throughout Marchon's history.

FIRST WORD: THE LEGACY OF MARCHON AND AL BERG

NOT LONG AGO, an optical industry pundit offered me this opinion: "The modern optical business was informed by three events—the creation of Lenscrafters, the creation of Warby Parker and the rise of Marchon Eyewear."

Coincidentally, I entered the industry as a trade publication editor at the same time the company that would eventually become Marchon was being brought to life by its three collaborative creators—Larry Roth, Jeff White and Al Berg.

Reflecting back on that brief period in optical history, the emergence of Marchon—the result of a series of somewhat controversial partnership break-ups followed by dramatic, new unions—was of itself not terribly significant. It was yet another eyewear company opening its doors in an environment where there were many eyewear companies.

But the Marchon story was unique. That three 30-year-old guys would have the courage and confidence to start an eyewear company with the intention of taking it to the top of the industry—and succeed—was very compelling. That they did it in a relatively short period of time only made the story that much richer.

As one picked it apart, the Marchon saga was very evidently replete with anomalous back stories. For one thing, there was no traditional hierarchy, just a kind of flat organization chart. There were the three extremely accessible owners and there was everybody else; and even the owners operated as equals—each was a co-president, at least early on. And to a great extent, ego didn't get in the way. They believed in management by argument, but when the arguing was done, it was only the best solution for the company that mattered.

The partners were incredibly complementary to each other. Larry ran the sales force, Jeff handled infrastructure (from the design and execution of Marchon's headquarters to its computer system to its distribution center), and Al was the business manager, and as was proved over time, the visionary. Their worldviews sort of balanced out too. As was told to me by a close Marchon associate: "If they were talking about buying chairs, Jeff would want to spend $1,000 a chair; Larry would want to go with $20 a chair; and Al would weigh the two options and come in at $200."

In the spring of 2018, I contacted Al to gauge his interest in helping me write the Marchon story.

"You know, it's funny you bring that up," he said. "A few people have suggested to me that I write a book."

What Al fully knew was that, as a notorious procrastinator, the chances of his producing a book without assistance were nil. So we began the project that would eventually lead to the words you're now reading.

We logged over fifteen hours of recorded conversations, and I compiled at least another fifteen of interviews with the employees, colleagues and competitors who knew Al and Marchon best. Their assessments and recollections were remarkably similar. And they always included expressions of awe, affection and admiration for Al. As Marty Fox, Marchon's one-time COO, told me: "Al made you feel proud to work there."

I knew when we began that Al was battling cancer, although we hardly ever discussed it. For the better part of the ten months that followed, he maintained a surprisingly cheerful demeanor and would typically answer "pretty good!" when I asked him how he felt.

Sometimes during our discussions, Al would wax a bit philosophical. He would in those circumstances often come up with a spontaneous metaphor or expression to better explain his attitude about a particular event or situation. We were talking about motivation, for example, and he wanted to underscore the distinction between the "Marchon view" on the subject and the views of others.

"Are you just making a living, or are you making a difference?" he casually said, possibly not quite realizing its fuller meaning. To Al, making a difference meant playing for futures and seeing the big picture, as opposed to simply worrying about today's sales. But truly making a difference could be so much more, as it was for him. Hence, that became the title of our book.

Shortly after 2019 began, it was obvious that Al's health was failing. He sounded less energetic when we spoke and he was explicit about wanting to get this project done fast. Finally on Monday, March 11, 2019, surrounded by his family, Al quietly passed away at age 67.

Just a few days before his death, Al and his family called me to say that it was more than likely he would never see the book completed and that I should persevere with his family's help. I assured him that I would.

The words that follow are largely Al's, but with an underpinning of facts and memories from many others. On behalf of Al and myself, we are grateful to the following for their help and interest in the project: Larry Roth, Dave Chute, Marty Fox, Dave Padgett, Donna Rollins, Jim McGrann, Robert Feldman, Barry Lerner, Fred Humphrey, Giancarla Agnoli, Barry Ballen, Ed Buffington, Judi Blondell, Deb Ingino, Linda Laube, Marge Axelrad, Harvey Ross, Deb Rich, Henry Sand, Rob Lynch and of course the Berg family—Gayle, Carly and Jarret. (I would also like to extend a personal thanks to Jeff Hopkins for his editorial guidance and wisdom.)

Al believed in the power of words and ideas, he lived by them. He was especially fond of the words that follow, applied them in both his business and personal lives, and sincerely wanted them to appear in these pages. The Serenity Prayer…

God grant me the serenity
To accept the things I cannot change;
Courage to change the things I can;
And wisdom to know the difference.

—*Frank Giammanco*
Upper Saddle River, N.J.

CHAPTER 1

THE END OF SOMETHING, AND THE BEGINNING

IN THE EARLY spring of 1982, on the eve of the start of the OptiFair trade show in New York City, Michael Berl and Frank White, equal partners in the thriving Avant Garde Optics company, sat down to dinner in a Manhattan restaurant. When they were finished, the partnership was dissolved and Berl was poised to become the sole owner.

Frank and Michael had been at odds for some time. Their relationship started as supplier and customer—Frank was selling American-made eyewear to Michael, whose Optica Berl, an eighteen-store optical retail chain in Venezuela, led the industry in that country.

For years, Frank had sold U.S. eyewear and some imported brands in the domestic market but also outside U.S. borders through his company, Consolidated Optical, because he had a European sensibility (as a native of Hungary) and was multilingual.

Michael Berl had also migrated to the Americas from Europe after World War II, met his wife, Fritzy (whose well-to-do family had something of an optical background) and the rest is history. Ultimately, the Berl family became one of the wealthiest in Venezuela.

While Michael needed to carry the more utilitarian product that Frank sold him in his stores, his business was built on the fashion and styling of higher-priced European eyewear. As friends, he cajoled Frank about starting an eyewear importing company in the U.S. to sell this revolutionary European product to American retailers and eye doctors.

Michael knew that the market potential for this type of eyewear was huge and the American market was vast. He also knew that he wanted to diversify his investments outside of Venezuela.

So in 1969, shortly after Neil Armstrong walked on the moon, Michael Berl and Frank White opened a new kind of eyewear company in Lake Success, N.Y. that was built on the imported eyewear products of overseas manufacturers like Austria's Silhouette, and L'Amy of France, and most importantly Luxottica, of Agordo, Italy. These companies were all family-run.

They called the new distribution company Avant Garde (incidentally, the name of a Great Neck, N.Y. beauty salon frequented by Ruth White, Frank's wife and business advisor) and they opened their doors to the American marketplace.

At that time, there were a number of domestic eyewear manufacturers supplying optical retail with eyewear products that they made largely at their own factories—though they did not supply them directly. These companies dominated the U.S. industry, and the concept of importing European eyewear was very new. While Avant Garde was not the first to attempt to construct a company on imports, it very quickly became one of the most successful.

These companies broke with the time-honored distribution model of selling to the industry's wholesale channel which would, in turn, sell to their customers at retail. Typically, the average wholesale sales rep would carry many lines of domestic eyewear from myriad U.S. manufacturers as well as a number of other products. The customer base was also purchasing prescription eyeglass lenses from them (which was and still is the primary product of the optical wholesaler), and everything else, from equipment to tools to eyeglass cases. (This would ultimately be the undoing of domestic manufacturers, but more on that later.)

The new Avant Garde was managed by Frank with the assistance of Ruth, who had always been active in the family business. Then four years after opening, they were joined by their son, Jeff White, and son-in-law, Larry Roth.

For his part, Michael Berl returned to Venezuela to wait for the money to start rolling in.

Avant Garde took the optical business by storm, and many of their reps were reaping great sales for the company and great sales commissions for themselves. While Frank and Ruth ran the business, Jeff handled operations and infrastructure and Larry managed the sales force. Michael was viewed as a strategic partner—someone to provide connections and financing to the business.

In the summer of 1980, at age 28, I joined the company at Jeff's encouragement. I had graduated from Harvard Business School five years prior and immediately went to work at my father's business, Silver Lining Textiles, based in midtown Manhattan.

We sold components for cuffs and collars to shirt and blouse makers and to put it mildly, it was not an exciting business, as the industry was stagnant and thoroughly commoditized. In fact, Silver Lining was flagging, a victim of an environment where market shares could shift for a penny or less. I worked days, nights and weekends (On Saturdays, I'd have to stomp on the floor when I entered the office to let the mice know a human was there.)

One of my primary duties was pricing our products, as each order was basically customized. I'd have to calculate the price down to one-eighth of one cent, and this took about 60% of my time at work. Commodity textiles was lackluster, the profit margins were thin and the work dreary.

I had gone to high school in Great Neck with Jeff White and would see him occasionally. Whenever I ran into him he'd tell me about how Avant Garde was growing at an incredible pace, how the whole eyewear industry was dynamic and moving in new directions. At almost every meeting, he'd try to coax me to join the company.

My Harvard Business School education gave me the tools that typically belong only to companies like General Motors. I learned the "big company" perspective on business management, and how to fine-tune my analytical skills. Most significantly I learned the importance of having a vision for the business, and how vital it was to maintain it.

Harvard gave me something else, too: a certain cache with the business world, as if my degree were resume enough. He probably wouldn't have admitted it, but I think it impressed Jeff and became a key reason for him to continue courting me.

Finally, one day I asked him, "How much time do you spend in your business on pricing?"

"About two hours."

"Two hours a day?" I asked

"Two hours a year."

He explained to me that they reviewed their pricelists once a year to determine pricing for the following year for ALL their customers, and that the whole process took about two hours. That resonated with me very positively. If I didn't have to spend the bulk of my time pricing products I could do more interesting stuff, like marketing. The job also offered twice as much as I was making at Silver Lining and freed me from the terrible daily commute to Manhattan (and the mice).

So I took Jeff up on his offer and became Avant Garde's first Vice President of Marketing and Business Development. Unlike the textiles business, the eyewear industry was dynamic, growing and full of energy. I loved the product, loved the business environment and very soon fell in love with the company I had joined.

With Jeff in charge of infrastructure—computer systems, WATS lines, shipping systems—areas of the company for which he had an unrivaled talent, and Larry managing the sales force, everything that was left over essentially went to me.

It was understood that Jeff was being groomed to run the company, and that caused him to sometimes make decisions unilaterally, often without informing the general management (his parents). When I started on a Monday morning, I bumped into Frank White, whom I knew from my high school days in Great Neck, and we started shooting the breeze. After about twenty minutes, Frank looked at me and said, "Don't you have to be at work?"

My immediate job at Avant Garde was to assist with the company's move from the offices in Lake Success to a huge, modern facility in Port Washington, N.Y. in September, 1980. Jeff had supervised the design of a 127,000 sq. ft. facility that included the latest distribution and shipping technology, computerization throughout and a customer service department that was unlike any other in the optical industry.

Avant Garde was an amazing business. It defied all the basic rules of eyewear procurement and distribution in the U.S. at that time. In addition to featuring only imported European eyewear products, the company employed a field sales organization to call on optometrists and opticians directly, an approach that very few players in the competitive arena were using at the time.

I reveled in the opportunities that Avant Garde presented to me. I was able to develop my first marketing program at AG, which we called the "Rimless Attack". Rimless eyewear was flying off the shelves at that time, thanks in no small part to the competitive power of Logo Paris Nylor Rimless eyewear, a product division of the French company, Essilor.

We looked to Luxottica and they came up with some really beautiful rimless frames. This was the first time that Avant Garde had put together a marketing program, and it was one of my first efforts—a great marketing attack, specifically targeted at a single eyewear category. We had identified a market that was working, with a product category that was working, and we went for it. Ironically, that campaign took place probably six months before we left Avant Garde.

Unfortunately, an enmity between Frank and Michael started to percolate. Michael wanted more control over the business, a better financial return as the business was not generating much in the way of dividends, and a job for his son, Carlos, who had been educated at New York University and wanted a career in the U.S. He was also growing apprehensive about the expense of constructing the new facility in Port Washington, which was in fact over budget.

Frank was starting to feel stifled by Michael's efforts to become more involved. Soon, the tensions were impacting others beyond just the two principal partners. On a buying trip to Italy, Frank and Ruth, along with Michael and his wife, Fritzy, were visiting the Luxottica showroom in Agordo, Italy.

Fritzy tried on what was known as a half-eye, a frame style for reading glasses. "That's not how you wear a half-eye!" Ruth apparently said to her, setting off a huge argument. Ruth White was an excellent and forward-thinking business woman (she hired the industry's first female sales rep and the first African-American), but not everyone knew how to handle her out-sized personality, Fritzy included.

Though any small incident could have rocked the fragile partnership at that time, it was the argument in Luxottica's showroom that served as the turning point. After that, things unfolded rapidly. One Monday a short time after their New York City dinner, Michael came to the office with a sizable check. Before the day was through, Frank and Ruth were gone.

Jeff and Larry determined that they needed to leave as well, and did so not more than twenty-four hours later. I was the last member of the management team to tender my resignation. Being analytical by nature, I wanted to step back and study the situation—but I didn't do so for long. Within a day or two, I followed my friends and co-workers out the door.

It was Michael Berl's objective to stabilize the company from a management perspective, but for the near term he realized that the people making day-to-day decisions and performing the tasks that make the business go were still in place. Eventually, he made a bold move to bring Avant Garde the stability it needed and change the trajectory of the company forever.

In the meantime, Jeff, Larry and I were trying to figure out what to do next. We had agreed that whatever we did, we'd do it together because we felt we made a great team. We started to look at businesses in other industries. For example, we considered buying a book distributor in Brooklyn and a tile company. But inevitably we'd circle back to what we believed we knew best, where our relationships were strongest, and which offered us the greatest opportunity to grow, and grow fairly rapidly—eyewear.

We quickly determined that we would start a company to rival Avant Garde. We would create an eyewear distribution business built on imported European eyewear. As we had done prior, we would work with several quality factories although only one would be our chief supplier.

Surprising as it was, with the exception of Frank White, we as Avant Garde's managers, including Ruth, did not have a non-competition agreement. We were happy to make Michael Berl aware of that and offered to sign non-competes for a price.

Michael refused, saying, "Please feel free to compete."

It didn't take us long to assemble a list of about ten European eyewear makers who could fit the bill. Not surprisingly, Luxottica was at the top of our list.

Luxottica was the creation of Leonardo Del Vecchio, a Milanese metals worker who was introduced to the eyewear business by the numerous clients he served in the Cadore region of Italy, all eyewear makers themselves. He started with his own small factory in the Agordo region, on land the local government had given him for free as an incentive to stimulate area employment. His brand very quickly became one of the leaders and ultimately led to his export relationship with Avant Garde.

Del Vecchio had become a major supplier to Avant Garde, representing more than 50% of its sales, and we knew his company and products well.

That spring, we decided to attend two major European trade fairs in Cologne, Germany and Milan, Italy. All the factories we wished to interview would be there, including Luxottica.

We met with Leonardo at the Milan show and told him of our intention to start a U.S. eyewear business similar to Avant Garde. While he was Avant Garde's major supplier, we knew as did he that there was no contractual agreement between the two. Michael Berl, we discovered, was also aware of this.

We provided him with a business plan that outlined an equal ownership scenario between Luxottica and the three of us—we didn't have a company name yet—and he assured us that he'd review it and get back to us before the trade show was done.

Soon after, Leonardo met with Michael Berl and advised him that 1) Avant Garde did not have a contract with Luxottica, and 2) that we had offered him 50% of our new company to be our chief supplier. Michael promptly offered him 50% of Avant Garde, a much more lucrative offer as they were generating revenue and we weren't.

In a follow-up meeting with Del Vecchio, he told us of Berl's offer and also expressed concerns about our new company.

"I looked at your projections for your first year," he said. "And you're estimating Luxottica sales at about one-third of what they are in the U.S. right now. The U.S. represents about half of my worldwide production and I can't risk that."

We did what any other fledgling entrepreneurs would do: we offered him 51% of the company, which would make him the ultimate decision maker.

The negotiating didn't end there, however. Upon hearing of our latest offer, Michael Berl told Leonardo that if he partnered with him now, he would have the right to buy Avant Garde outright in three years—at a price that they would set in stone that day in May of 1982.

Del Vecchio had played his cards well. He leveraged his position with us to get the best deal he could from Michael. For his part, Michael managed to stabilize the company, and put it on a path of unprecedented growth never before seen by any U.S. eyewear distributor.

Undaunted, our next stop was Silhouette, the Linz, Austria company operated by the Schmied family, who had roots in the business as opticians for many years. Their eyewear was unique and utilized various metals in new ways. It drew the attention early on of many celebrities, including Queen Elizabeth.

Coincidentally, their Italian distributor had been Luxottica and the two companies had a huge falling out when Silhouette allegedly discovered that Leonardo was copying some of their most popular styles and selling them at a significantly lower price.

When we met with the family, of course, we couldn't resist telling them who the new partner was at Avant Garde, causing them to immediately begin the process of terminating their distribution relationship.

Silhouette, we believed, would make a good supplier to our new company, but their higher price-point would make it difficult to depend on them broadly. Also, the Schmieds believed they'd be better off tackling the U.S. market on their own, with an American footprint that they maintain to the present.

Finally, there was one other factory that had intrigued us, another family-run Italian firm called Marcolin. The Marcolin story very much paralleled Luxottica's: both were founded in the early 1960s by strong patriarchs (in Marcolin's case, it was Giovanni Marcolin Coffen); both were headquartered in nearby regions in the northern Italian province of Belluno (Marcolin was based in Longarone, Italy); and both were known for quality eyewear and efficient production.

But in many ways, Marcolin was an under-appreciated and underutilized factory. Known for their excellent work in creating metal eyewear, the company had arranged a distribution agreement with another global supplier called Optyl, based in Germany but with a substantial beachhead in the northeastern U.S. Marcolin supplied a metal collection to Optyl under their popular brand, terri brogan, but as with so many partnerships in the eyewear industry, theirs was somewhat fractious. Apparently, Optyl didn't want the Marcolin brand on the eyewear they sold, and that didn't sit well with Giovanni.

When we showed up at the Marcolin stand toward the close of the Italian trade fair MIDO, Giovanni was anticipating our arrival.

"What took you so long?" he said. "I've been waiting for you."

Apparently, Marcolin's export director had been assigned the task of getting in touch with us prior to MIDO to set up an appointment but failed to do so, a misstep that he came to regret. But it told us that Giovanni was as inclined toward doing business with us as we were with him.

Marcolin was an excellent fit in many ways. The company was well-respected throughout the industry, and they were positioned to have a much bigger presence in the U.S. market than Optyl provided.

In fact, upon our closing the deal with Marcolin, it was determined that Optyl would cease distributing the terri brogan metals line by year-end '82. This meant that we would have to service that customer base and deal with issues like returns. It also meant that we would be taking over Marcolin's metals distribution.

In our new business plan, we determined that there should be three companies operating synergistically. One would be called Marcolin USA, and it would be owned jointly by the Italian company and us, to make and sell Marcolin products. A second company would be owned exclusively by me, Larry and Jeff, and its purpose would be to acquire eyewear from other factories, such as Calamand (owned by brothers Michele and Jean Pierre Calamand) and Grasset (owned by Pierre Grasset) from Oyonnax, France. They both supplied us with acetate frames to diversify our product mix.

Lastly there would be a single U.S. company that would maintain a sales force, handle marketing and procure the products of the other two companies. At that point it didn't have a name, but we knew that it would be the primary brand customers would come to know.

As we prepared for the launch, we consulted closely with Giovanni on product development and delivery. As our relationship progressed over the years, he came to realize that there was much more to the U.S. market than he or the Marcolin company fully understood, so he appointed one of his twin sons, Mauricio, a marketing major, to relocate to the U.S. and work with us as part of our team (it also allowed him by Italian law to avoid military service). The other twin, Cirillo, majored in economics and hence wound up in finance and administration.

Of course, we needed money to execute our plans, and we were fortunate to receive at least some of it from Ruth White. Ruth provided us with a $1 million loan. Frank was prohibited from funding our business because of the provisions of his non-competition agreement, but Ruth was free to do as she pleased—a bit of an oversight on the part of Michael Berl.

With Ruth's $1 million we were able to secure a loan from Citibank for an additional million. We immediately made some decisions to put the money to work that ultimately assured our success, although others might have thought them risky.

Computerization of small businesses was just starting to really take off, and we knew we had to follow that path. We had no customers, and for that matter, no product to sell, but we knew that a computer system would inevitably be a necessity. It was a very expensive decision, the purchase requiring 40% of our seed money.

But we also knew that starting with a manual business management system would mean more work and more effort when we did go automated down the road (presuming we were still in business).

Others undoubtedly would have played it more conservatively, but we were thoroughly convinced of two things: 1) we needed to make decisions based on long-term objectives, and 2) we were going to succeed, and for that reason the computer investment was a gamble worth taking.

Through a real estate friend we obtained our first headquarters, an office and warehouse space in Plainview, N.Y., just off the Long Island Expressway. Another friend "lent" us some clerical staff from his personnel ranks and we were off to start assembling a team.

Eventually, there were twelve "inside," or headquarters-based people, including we three owners. This group included our warehouse manager, customer service personnel and accounting help.

Our next recruitment task was a little harder—building the sales team. We knew that, for many reasons, we couldn't simply start raiding Avant Garde, although a few AG salespeople did cross our paths.

Dave Padgett was an experienced eyewear salesman whom Larry and Frank had pursued while at Avant Garde. Dave was a southeast-based sales manager for a German eyewear company called Menrad, and was on the verge of joining AG when the company got sold. As Dave says, he was "left at the altar."

But by the summer of '82, Dave was once again on Larry's mind; he called him and pitched him on our new, nameless company. Dave was surprised but very intrigued. After he heard Larry's pitch, and despite the fact that he was doing quite well at Menrad, Dave chose to "hitch his wagon" to our nascent company on the hunch that we were going places.

He then proceeded to recruit other quality reps from the ranks of Menrad and a few other companies. The rep network in the eyewear field was always pretty tight, so when word got out about a new company or opportunity, it spread quickly. It didn't take Larry and Dave long to fill in a few more gaps on the sales team.

A pair of Avant Garde veterans, a couple named Barry and Nina Lerner, were excited about joining us also. Based in Florida, they had incredible command of that market and knew the customer base well. But when they signed on with us, they informed us that it was their intention to go west, all the way to the Pacific Ocean and Southern California—where they did not know a single account.

Still, we had faith in their talents and green-lighted the move, and in their first year their sales exceeded $500,000.

In total, we had built a team of twenty-four people, twelve in sales and twelve in the office. All the pieces were falling into place, but we still didn't have a name for the new company and we were just months away from our scheduled launch date.

We hired a marketing agency called Arthur Kramer Advertising and gave them the assignment of creating a name for this new business. We wanted it to somehow or other convey fashion, have something of a European feel to it and be no more than two or three syllables long. We also wanted a name that would be easily remembered and easily recognized through a distinct and very different logo treatment.

The agency, however, was consistently striking out. They'd come up with names like Chi-Chi and C'est Bon, just horrible stuff, and we were getting frustrated. Finally, in November, they came up with Marchon and it clicked with us immediately.

I remember phoning my mom and dad to tell them the news about the company's new name and get their opinion of it. My father's reaction truly surprised me.

"You've taken one of our family names for your company," he said.

"What do you mean?"

"Marshon was your grandmother's maiden name...Kate Marshon."
That was all I needed to solidify the decision.

Marchon sounded fashionable, sophisticated and European. It also complemented the name of our partner company, Marcolin.

We soon had the distinctive logo we were looking for: black type in an almost handwritten script, and the "O" of Marchon a solid, red dot. The dot became an iconic symbol, much like the Nike "swoosh," and we maintained it in much of our marketing and trade show presentations.

By December, we were just about ready to begin the race. We had even contacted the organizers of the OptiFair trade show, which took place every spring at the New York Hilton in Manhattan. But at four months out, the 1983 show was already completely booked.

We went to the show site in midtown Manhattan and looked around. The show basically occupied a large ballroom space. Immediately outside the ballroom was a fairly wide hallway and the elevator bank. That's what we wanted! A unique space, outside of the fair's conventional exhibit area but right at the entranceway where everyone could see it. A perfect presentation for an eyewear company's premiere.

The show organizers balked at the idea at first, but then came around when they realized we were quite serious and had the money to back it up. As we had anticipated, the debut of Marchon was the hit of the show.

As 1982 ended, we brought our group of twenty-four employees together at the Plainview office for our first ever company meeting. We shared with them our aspirations, our vision for the company, our ambition to build a great business for the long term and not just sell eyeglass frames day-to-day. It quickly became obvious that our enthusiasm was contagious. The other twenty-one people on our team wanted to adopt the Marchon philosophy as their own. And in those moments the seeds of our future success were planted.

We officially opened our doors on January 1, 1983. Soon the orders started coming in—slowly at first, but then more briskly. But more importantly, within a few months the reorders began to flow and the phones began to ring. We knew fairly quickly that we had a hit.

But unbeknownst to us on that January 1st, three other companies were also creating some fanfare. Charmant, a Japanese company, opened its distribution center in New Jersey. Silhouette, which had split from Avant Garde, became its own U.S. distributor.

And Avant Garde itself, now operated by Carlos Berl, son of Michael, and Claudio Del Vecchio, son of Leonardo, launched a new corporate division called BerDel. It was immediately clear to us that they would be our most challenging competitor for many years to come.

Our business grew more and more robust, and by about midyear it became apparent that we were going to beat our budget numbers. We closed 1983 with approximately $3.8 million in revenue.

Over the course of that first year, some things changed and we became wiser about the business. With the challenges of assembling a good infrastructure for Marchon now behind us, Jeff decided to leave the company. He would leave and return several times throughout the life of Marchon.

As for me, I was one of the fortunate few in life who had found his professional destiny and never looked back. It would be a twenty-five year journey that helped to define who I was and who I would become.

CHAPTER 2

THE ENTREPRENEURIAL TRIUMVIRATE

WHEN LARRY, JEFF and I decided to launch the company that would eventually become Marchon, we did so on a handshake basis. Although we hadn't been working together for very long, we were like-minded in many respects, each with a strong work ethic, a desire to succeed and a deep respect for each other. We were also, all three, natural entrepreneurs.

For me, entrepreneurship was embedded in my DNA. My father had his own business, as did my grandfather (who was also an attorney).

My family wasn't poor by any means, but we had no sense of entitlement. I was taught the value of a dollar and throughout my teenage years I had a number of part-time jobs.

As a kid growing up in the well-to-do community of Great Neck, Long Island, I tended to be on the shy side which was a bit of a liability in terms of achieving my goals.

When the time came for me to begin my undergraduate career at Syracuse University, my folks drove me to the airport and my mom said something to me which has stuck with me. In fact, I used her comment at Marchon on many occasions.

"When you get off that plane," she said to me, "no one will know who you are or anything about you. You can be anything you want to be."

I took her advice immediately to heart, and by the time I set foot on the Syracuse campus, I was determined to be different.

When I got to the dorm, for example, the dorm director told us we had to elect a floor president. I nudged the guy next to me and said, "Hey, nominate me." He did and I won. And that for me was a turning point from introvert to extrovert.

I was an accounting major and admittedly not a very good student. But that didn't matter, because the education I was truly receiving was the result of the many activities I had outside of the classroom. I became president of one of the fraternities. The school operated a "student corporation," and when I started to run it, I had free reign.

After Syracuse, I applied to Harvard Business School and was accepted. Harvard made an enormous difference in my life—it allowed me to hone my analytical skills and also broadened my view of what the world could look like.

Of course, I had never been a CEO when I got to Avant Garde, but I discovered two incredible mentors in Frank and Ruth White. What I learned from them in the nearly two years of my tenure would help to carry me through the next twenty-five.

At the outset, we three knew we wanted to be in business together, but what that business was and what it would look like remained an unknown in the spring of 1982. We would all three share in the equity of whatever asset we created or bought. Had we started a company in a brand new industry, that ownership would have been divided into even thirds. Had it been an optical business, Jeff and Larry would have received larger percentages, and if that optical business involved a relationship with Luxottica, they'd receive more equity still. (As time went by the percentages of ownership changed and I—for a number of reasons—finally wound up with significant equity.)

We also determined from the start that our titles should be identical—co-president. We truly believed that each of us brought something unique but of equal value to the game and therefore a hierarchical management structure was unnecessary. In an industry dominated by very strong-willed, entrepreneurial company chiefs, this was considered unusual.

But for as much as we were very compatible, we were also very different.

Larry was very much "by the book," methodical, purposeful, serious. In our meetings, he brought to us every important conservative principle upon which a company is run. How much money do we have? What's our best investment?

His primary role at Marchon was management of the sales force, which he did effectively through a network of very passionate regional managers. He had an incredible memory (some referred to him as a human CRM system) and a great analytical skill. He knew every rep's name (quite a feat when our sales force exceeded three-hundred), but more than that he knew the composition of their territories, who were the standout accounts, for reasons both good and bad, and how well (or not so well) each rep performed with each type of account.

Jeff was the exact opposite. Where Larry was a conservative, practical thinker, Jeff was flamboyant and frequently over-the-top. We'd be debating making a certain investment and Larry would protest the size of the expenditure while Jeff would want to do it first-class, whether we had the resources or not.

Money was of little significance to Jeff and he could be generous to a fault—at company dinner functions it wasn't unusual for him to arbitrarily tip wait staff with one hundred dollar bills. Or to send a $50,000 check to some Iowa farmer who was down on his luck that he'd seen on TV.

I like to think that I was the moderating force for both; I'd advise caution when I thought it necessary or advise risk when I thought it was worthwhile. I sometimes imagined Jeff and Larry on either end of a seesaw, with me right in the middle.

As a consequence, there were no real battles of ego. I had what I believe was a healthy ego; Larry to some extent suppressed his. But we were all interested in getting the best answers and achieving the best outcomes for the company. Hence, we all fell into our natural roles in pursuit of those goals.

Although there was great synergy among us, we would of course have occasional disagreements. Sometimes loud ones.

We had acquired nine acres of commercial land in Melville, N.Y., not far from our first offices, and in 1988, with Jeff's stewardship and creativity we completed a brand new Marchon headquarters, featuring state-of-the-art facilities and design. Jeff had included a huge, triangular conference table—each side about twenty feet long—almost as a metaphor for our partnership.

Each of us would sit on our side of the triangle and often have fairly animated conversations, so animated in fact that the employees outside the conference room were certain that one of us had killed the others. But when the yelling and debating was over, we'd emerge from the conference room as though nothing had happened.

One of the things I tend to think about our partnership is that we were authentic. We could argue and disagree but remain confident that we'd come out of it with the same steadfast respect for each other—a claim that few partnerships can genuinely make.

The new headquarters at 35 Hub Drive in Melville was a great achievement for Jeff. Not only was it extremely modern and uniquely designed, Jeff had made sure to build in tremendous operating efficiencies and new technologies. For example, our warehouse featured an almost mistake-proof system for fulfilling orders, both small and large.

And Jeff did something that until that time was unprecedented—he brought two of our major vendors, AT&T and IBM, together to make it possible for a customer service rep to review a customer's profile on the computer screen upon immediately receiving his phone call.

Often, we would over-build or over-invest in order to plant the seeds for growth. If we needed to build out one of our business assets to accommodate an additional 5,000 customers, we'd make it to accommodate 10,000, a great way to plan for the future but admittedly not great for profit margins.

Regardless, I think this was our comparative advantage, being able to use smart judgment and take informed risks. We were operating in an environment where smart entrepreneurs were looking for security as opposed to taking risks. From my perspective we weren't taking chances, we were betting on growth. I believe you can't build a big company without that instinct.

Jeff certainly had that instinct, maybe a little too much of it. Where Larry would often take the more conservative approach, Jeff would want to go all out. I used to say about Jeff that he was something of a Howard Hughes—incredibly smart, even brilliant…and nuts.

Larry and I had families and tended toward more conservative lifestyles. Jeff, on the other hand, was single and by his own admission a little immature, a perennial teenager. He was the quintessential party animal, often going out to New York clubs until the early hours of the morning. However, Jeff did bring some of his sense of fun and his party personality to the corporate culture and people appreciated that. He loved sales meetings for example, and he made sure there was an element of fun to them.

In that regard, his role at Marchon was perfectly suited to him. He'd come alive when faced with a new infrastructure challenge, such as integrating a new computer system or designing a new office building. But he had little patience for, or interest in, the day-to-day operations of Marchon. When he wasn't needed, he would take an occasional hiatus from the company (what I called "hibernation") and pursue other businesses or opportunities, including month-long trips with friends to Hawaii or other exotic hideaways.

In some ways, this periodic idleness was Jeff's undoing. He would sometimes become bored, and he lived for sensation, which made for a dangerous and self-destructive relationship with drugs and alcohol. Yet when he was on his game, he was on his game. He would go through seventy-page contracts with meticulous precision, catching one typo among thousands of words. He memorized hundreds of phone numbers. He was quite capable of navigating the highest levels of detail.

We had an unwritten rule about decision making. A two-thirds majority would advance a garden-variety decision, but a unanimous vote was required for a big, life-changing decision. In the late 1990s, for example, a very smart, savvy investor named Martin Franklin had entered the optical marketplace with the intention of making a number of deals. He came to us with the opportunity to make an acquisition, the sports protective eyewear company called Bolle, for $75 million.

Larry and I liked the idea. It would put Marchon in a new product category and possibly help us expand our customer base. Jeff, believe it or not, was adamantly against it as it was not our core competency. Ultimately his "nay" vote shot the deal down, and deservedly so. In retrospect, it probably would have bankrupted the company at a very formative stage in its lifecycle.

Jeff's death on November 30, 2005 at the unforgivable age of 54 was sudden and tragic. Drugs had destroyed him. We probably should have seen it coming. His passing impacted me in a number of ways. I had lost a wonderful friend and a generous partner. It also made me think that, over time, maybe I wasn't there for him as a friend as much as I could have been. Predictably, his death didn't impact the day-to-day operation of Marchon (his role in IT was filled admirably by Jim McGrann who became CIO in 1999). But it did change the soul and culture of the company.

Ironically, his passing took place on the day of our annual holiday party, and we thought long and hard about whether or not to hold it. We finally determined that we should—certainly Jeff always enjoyed a party. One of our international managers at the time, Andy Skitmore, a U.K. native, mentioned that his tradition in the event of a death was for family and friends to give the deceased a standing ovation. And that's what we did to honor Jeff.

By the time he left, all the tough and major decisions for Marchon had been made by the triumvirate. The Marchon philosophy was in place, and Larry and I were pretty much running the company.

We had at that point and for some time prior abandoned the co-president titles. Larry managed the domestic sales organization. I became de facto CEO. I have mentioned that I had never held that position before, but I believed that two things prepared me to do it: my observations of Frank and Ruth White for my two years at Avant Garde, and my Harvard education. I would be tested in the role on several occasions but always tried to maintain my cool and move us forward. As long as I was receiving reliable information from the various members of our team, I was always confident that we could surmount any hurdle.

Avant Garde proved to be a significant influence on the three of us as we nurtured Marchon into existence. At the time of AG's inception, there were few eyewear companies selling European product directly to optical dispensers. From our perspective, there was no other way to do it.

The Avant Garde that existed prior to its complete acquisition by Luxottica in 1985 provided our early road map. The company that ultimately became Luxottica U.S. served as our compass.

Keeping Luxottica within our sights kept us very focused. It inspired us to build a great company, not just be a bunch of guys selling eyeglass frames at a trade show as many eyewear suppliers were doing.

Not to mix too many metaphors, but I used to think of Luxottica as the motor boat and Marchon as the water skier right behind it. Wherever Lux went, we followed, always presuming that those were the moves world-class companies made.

More specifically, it was Leonardo Del Vecchio who was our inspiration, or certainly mine. He was a fierce competitor but also, I later realized, as much a mentor as anyone I had known. He was capable of being ruthless when he felt he needed to be, and could make dramatic decisions that affected a thousand employees without blinking an eye. He was able to do things that would make me, or another manager, cringe. But that was the key to who he is and why he became successful.

He also, arguably, operated as a management team of one, where we obviously shared in Marchon's management and even extended those responsibilities to many of our lieutenants. It was my sort of dubious assumption that when Del Vecchio got up in the morning, he thought about new ways to conquer the world, whereas when I got up in the morning, I was thinking of ways to move the company forward.

Nonetheless, he had the vision and ability to make bold moves when others would not.

He was the first to sign a global, "A" list brand in Giorgio Armani, with Marchon countering by signing Calvin Klein. He was also among the first to add on a second sales force to launch the BerDel brand. We also eventually went with the multiple sales force strategy. And as a global company, Luxottica impressed upon me the need to have a global footprint if we were to be a major player.

Most significantly, in 1996 he dared to do something that few had even dreamed of in the eyewear business: he acquired the high-visibility and somewhat controversial optical chain called Lenscrafters (actually Precision Lenscrafters back then), putting Luxottica in the retail business from that point on. It was a move that challenged Luxottica's wholesale business and customer base.

When the news came down, I was traveling to Dallas for a manager's meeting. I remember walking into the room and immediately saying, "Today, the world as we know it has changed." (Of course, the comment was confined to the optical world.)

In this instance, we had no intention of following Del Vecchio into optical retailing, but we did recognize that the Lenscrafters brand had a high level of consumer awareness. At around the same time, or just prior, we began a more aggressive consumer advertising strategy with some of our most distinctive products like Flexon memory metal eyewear. (It's been said that Luxottica decided to buy Lenscrafters upon seeing the impact of our Flexon TV commercials, realizing the power of consumer branding.)

Throughout my years at Marchon, Luxottica loomed large and never failed to make news with unexpected ventures.

In late 1999, Bausch & Lomb, primarily known as a contact lens and pharmaceuticals supplier, had decided to spin out its venerated Ray-Ban sunglasses division. Candidly, the brand had not been managed well and Ray-Ban was available at every retail outlet from drug stores to gas stations, often at prices below wholesale. The product's quality had declined as well, as the manufacturing facility in Mexico was using antiquated equipment and substandard materials.

Bain Capital Ventures was interested in making a play for Ray-Ban, and they came to us at Marchon to serve as the operating arm. Of course, the opportunity excited us.

Ray-Ban at that time was valued at $400 million, and that's what Bain offered B&L. We were aware that there were other bidders and that one of them was Del Vecchio, who wanted Ray-Ban a bit more than Bain did. He wound up bidding $640 million, effectively shutting down all the other suitors.

I sometimes think that if Marchon had obtained Ray-Ban it would have changed our culture—possibly for better, possibly for worse.

Of course, Luxottica closed the deal and Del Vecchio once again surprised the eyewear world by taking Ray-Ban off the market—closing down 13,000 points of sale for six months—so that the distribution quagmire could be cleaned up. He also closed down the Mexico plant (though he promised B&L that he wouldn't).

Several years later, I asked Leonardo why he was willing to pay so much for Ray-Ban (he actually did negotiate the price down a little, but nowhere near $400 million). He simply replied, "Because it was worth it."

And indeed, for Luxottica it was. Today, it's arguably the most recognized eyewear brand in the world, with sales exceeding two billion euro and thirty-million units worldwide, 27% of Luxottica's annual sales and 5% of the world's total eyewear market.

While I think it's safe to say that Marchon would have done a good job with Ray-Ban, we certainly didn't have the resources to achieve that kind of success. At least at that time we didn't.

My admiration for Luxottica and Del Vecchio obviously did not prevent us from competing. But there was a rumor floating around that Leonardo had told his U.S. team to "go easy" on us, as he had great respect for the Whites and admired what we had done to help Avant Garde become his launching pad. Ironically, I have probably only met and spoken with Leonardo maybe five times over the years, and then only briefly. But his impact on Marchon, and me, was indelible. And for our triumvirate, it helped us fine-tune our focus, keep our eye on the prize and build a great, talented and equally focused team.

CHAPTER 3

BUILDING A TEAM, CREATING A CULTURE

FROM THE BEGINNING, we were always a "people" company. As I mentioned, Marchon started with two dozen people—twelve inside (administration, operations, marketing, etc.) and twelve outside (sales). This included the three principals, me, Larry and Jeff (or ALJ as we were later known).

But within those first twenty-four employees resided an optimism, a desire and a passion to assure that Marchon would succeed. And that started with the three of us.

One of the things I learned in the process of building the company is that good people attract other good people. After we opened our doors, word quickly got around that we were hiring and that Marchon was a good place to work. And as we grew and delegated some hiring responsibility, those people would ultimately recruit others with the same personality traits. As the company continued to expand throughout the years, these people helped to form a culture that then duplicated itself throughout the world among thousands of employees.

We never wanted to make team-building a complicated process, and did not allow any form of bias or influence of ego to affect it. Male, female, young, old—it didn't matter so long as the individual was smart, hard-working and committed to succeeding. (If the first question a job candidate asked is "What's your vacation policy?" you'd certainly think twice about hiring them.)

And while having experience was a plus, particularly for the sales team, it wasn't a prerequisite. For example, we hired a woman named Sheila Weinberg, who was married to one of our local sales reps, and made her the warehouse manager despite the fact that she hadn't managed a warehouse before. Nonetheless, she was one of our greatest successes.

I took a great deal of pride in hiring or promoting smart, talented people. Ron Kitt, the head of Marchon's global distribution, is one of the company's most important executives. I met him on the loading dock of a Pergament Home Center. Howie Nadler was a young guy working as a temple changer in the warehouse and became one of our most accomplished sales reps, contributing significantly to the success of Calvin Klein. Donna Rollins, who became our marketing head, was working at our ad agency, Arthur Kramer Advertising. And most famously, Giancarla Agnoli, who had been Marcolin's assistant export manager, ultimately took charge of our 100,000 sq. ft. Italian factory, distribution center and our entire Italian operation. It pleases me to say that there are many more such stories.

Admittedly, Marchon was not an easy place to work. We expected a great deal from everyone we hired, and we made that clear throughout the interview process. I would like to challenge job candidates by not asking the kinds of questions they would have expected in order to break down communication barriers and get them talking.

One tactic I often used was to turn the interview around and ask the candidate why I should *not* hire them. I'd explain that our company was very hands-on, that we had very high expectations for all new team members, and that I was not inclined to hire someone unless they were sure ours was the type of company and environment they wanted to work in. I'd point out that our work ethic was challenging and very fast-paced, that they shouldn't want this job unless they were ready for real change and commitment. If not that was okay too, and we'd all move on. It had to be the right fit—for them, for the company, for the team. In fact, the more I wanted a person, the harder I tried to convince them not to take the job.

At some point in Marchon's evolution, the hiring process would begin at the key manager level and I wouldn't take part until after they had narrowed the field. Generally, I had a pretty good idea if I wanted to hire someone. Often, it was someone I had targeted. Our key people would do the screening using the tactics I described, and then I'd be brought in to close the deal—which I did successfully about 99% of the time. It was my job to make the goal of working for the company a real "stretch" and if I hired someone, it would typically be a great ride for us all.

For those who made the cut, in some ways a new world opened up for them. I know that sounds corny and maybe a little bombastic, but I really do believe that we, collectively, contributed to an environment that allowed people to express themselves, take pride of authorship, work hard and play hard. We would, in our own words, "Marchonize" them, or immerse them in the Marchon culture.

A number of employees have told me over the years that there was something about the Marchon culture that made you want to work there, that we had created an *esprit de corps* that made our people feel like they were a part of a family. After all, we came from family companies where everybody stayed forever so we knew no other way to do it.

Every Thanksgiving season, a big, refrigerated truck would pull up to our Melville headquarters and deliver turkeys to everybody. Every summer we'd have a great picnic/barbeque on the property where the managers did all the cooking. Certainly we could have hired a service to come in and cater it, but we felt it was more personal, more fun (and definitely more cost-effective) for us to do it ourselves.

We did not stand on a lot of ceremony. We weren't jacket and tie guys—more jeans and sport shirts. Also, we were very accessible and practiced an open-door policy, a fact that some new hires found a little disconcerting, particularly supervisors. But I always wanted to hear what was going on, not to take anyone's side but to understand.

As Marchon flourished and new people were constantly joining our ranks, we realized that some of them probably came from cultures that deliberately maintained a lot of distance between management and staff. It amazed me as the boss that people wouldn't want to talk to me, or would choose their words very carefully. You had to be something of a psychologist to break open communication. But you've got to get your employees to talk if you're going to get the true story.

Now, it's a lot easier running a growing organization if you don't listen. It can be a little bit of a Pandora's Box when you do—you could get bad news as often as you got good news. Hence, there are managers who prefer not to listen. They'd rather the problem just disappear on its own, or the person reporting the problem just go away. From our perspective, particularly mine, that approach would be extremely counter-productive.

I was never keen on surprises. In 1997, for example, I learned that our warehouse people were exploring the idea of bringing in a union. This news upset me greatly. Like a lot of employers I believed that we had proven ourselves to our people many, many times, and a union was not necessary.

Distraught over the situation, I turned to a personal friend, Robert Feldman, and asked him to help us tackle this issue. I had known Robert and his wife for many years; he had a background in recruiting and personnel management and had also dealt with unions. He joined us as a consultant and instantly recognized that there was a communications breakdown between the warehouse employees and management, partly as a result of our not having installed a level of middle management which could serve as a bridge between the worker and the executive levels. Once we had that in place, the prospect of a union at Marchon disappeared. It reemerged several years later and was immediately dismissed. Robert, by the way, became our HR manager.

The union dilemma illustrated to me the importance of good, honest communication throughout the company. You don't want people burying problems and avoiding discussion. In order to manage effectively, you want and need the truth. Problems can be good things if they're presented in a timely and honest way. Otherwise, they fester and become larger, and less solvable.

In my capacity, eventually, as CEO of the company, it was incumbent upon me to set its tone and its character for everyone else. There were certain aphorisms that, though often unspoken, provided guidance for the whole company: the good of the company is paramount, and personal grievances or petty jealousies should be put aside; let's do the job today, but keep an eye on tomorrow (a trait, I believe, that distinguished us from much of our U.S. competition); execute with the goal of achieving perfection.

These were just some of the ideas that drove Marchon, and while I can't say that everyone on the team embraced them enthusiastically, I know that the majority of them did. And again, it was a cultural ethic that kept replicating itself. Just about every new hire brought with them the fundamentals of the Marchon philosophy, because the people who hired them would accept nothing less. We were very good at getting people who were very good.

Occasionally, we'd lose a good employee, and we'd look at it as a learning experience. There's always going to be turnover, but I believed that too much turnover indicated there was a problem and we needed to determine how to fix it. What could we have done differently? It often came down to a breakdown in communication.

We'd always prefer that they not leave and many of our people stayed a long time. But if their departure was inevitable, it was our philosophy that everyone has an obligation to themselves to achieve their potential, and if that meant leaving Marchon then so be it.

Interestingly, I came to realize that the people who were most successful—the ones who became the most "Marchonized"—were the ones who had a knack for entrepreneurship, meaning they could develop a plan and then execute that plan. Where we had the least success was often when we'd hire a person with a very corporate mentality. I called these people "maintainers" because they depended upon a plan or strategy already being in place that they could simply maintain.

That was not the Marchon way—you took your idea, sketched out your plan, argued for your plan with management, and then executed.

That was challenging for some, but very enticing for others, particularly industry people who were working for our competitors. In fact, as the Marchon story spread throughout the optical industry, many people would come to us for jobs—especially salespeople.

In any good consumer products company, a high-quality sales organization is fundamental to success. This is especially true in the competitive eyewear space, where the average retailer sees seven to ten reps per week.

As with a number of things, we were lucky in that we selected experienced salespeople early on who could attract other quality salespeople. Dave Padgett, whom I mentioned prior, was our first southeast regional sales manager and one of our original twenty-four employees. He had been with the German eyewear firm, Menrad, and brought us several great reps from that company. As the company expanded and we brought on more regional managers—like Henry Rothchild and Judi Blondell—they brought in still more high-caliber reps, the majority of them with strong customer franchises.

When pursuing a job, a salesperson is looking for several ingredients for their success: a solid product line, an emphasis on service, caring management, and compensation that they feel is warranted. I'd like to think we gave them that and in so doing kept the sales team stable. No one would jump ship simply for a few dollars.

We knew when we first started, for example, that prospective salespeople had the expectation that they would change jobs to make more money, and often did so, presuming that the right job and the right company would automatically result in more income. However that assumption is not valid for a new company that may not have have sought-after product lines and strong followings among retailers and their consumers right out of the gate.

The reality was that the salesperson that has a good relationship with their customer is the engine that drives initial success. We recognized that we had to reset expectations, that we were offering opportunities for salespeople who wanted to be treated fairly, backed by an organization that was dedicated to working very hard to help them succeed. We had to convey to them that unlike other eyewear suppliers who were known for letting their reps build territories only to see them divided up or taken away once they achieved their goals, we were in it with them to build the business together.

From the very beginning, we viewed our salespeople as we viewed the customer. They were our first touch-point with the actual customer and served as the customer's mouthpiece to communicate with us. And whatever intelligence they brought back we'd respond to immediately. We treated our customer service people in much the same way because they were an important touch-point, receiving orders from some customers several times per week. So it was our objective to provide excellent service to the customer and in so doing also satisfy the needs of the sales and customer service teams.

We did a very good job of sharing best practices among our team; we'd let our fifteen most experienced reps just sit in a room at our sales meetings and share what they knew, effectively downloading their brains to learn what is required to best service the customer. Then our inside team would create the materials necessary to execute those best practices. This went a long way in making our people truly feel like each was a part of this greater whole where everyone contributed.

One of the most critical things we needed our team to understand, and we emphasized it at every meeting or interaction with our salespeople, was this: a salesperson's job isn't complete when the product is shipped, but when it sells through.

Considering the very liberal return policies within our industry, if we were ultimately responsible for the products that didn't sell through, then it was our job to do the best we could to help our customers move them. A salesperson was to do anything and everything necessary to assist the customer in making the sale to their customer. Whether that meant providing the right marketing or presenting sales education to the staff, our people had to be good communicators and good educators. They had to deliver meaningful seminars and exceptional service. They had to reinvest in their sales territories, which might require their buying lunch or breakfast for the office and presenting a solid sales training program.

We thought a lot about the care and feeding of our sales force. We'd never ask them to do something that wasn't to their benefit. And we spent a lot of time thinking about innovative new tools and sales concepts that we could create to make their jobs easier.

It's a little ironic in retrospect, but we wound up hiring two different types of people: those who had heard about Marchon's success and wanted to embrace some of the new tools and methods that we made available, and those who had no interest in changing or adopting new ideas. It didn't mean they weren't successful, but they were frequently not our best salespeople.

Something that salespeople often didn't comprehend was that if you just depended upon the buyer looking into your frame bag and being bowled over, you'd be disappointed. The frames in your bag are similar to the ones they're already selling. The magic wasn't in the bag, it was in the person. Our sales resources would help that magic do great things.

That's not to say that a Marchon rep's job was idyllic. Frequently, we'd have to address internal challenges to our culture that were largely predicated on our rapid growth. In order to accommodate a continuously growing company, you have to look at your systems and business philosophies and—no matter how wedded you are to them—explore the need for change. In a company like Marchon very little stayed the same for very long.

For example, we had gotten to a point in the early 1990s where we were actually managing two big companies—Marchon and Marcolin. Each deserved to be a company unto itself, with a separate sales force. This was a trend that was starting to emerge in the U.S. industry; as I mentioned before, Avant Garde had done this for their BerDel product line.

I knew that having more than one salesperson calling on the account would significantly improve our service, and our sales performance. But I also knew that there would be a lot of disgruntled salespeople if we made that move. And though it was a hard decision, I felt strongly that adding a second sales team was in the best long-term interests of the company.

The success of the concept was proved, albeit by managers at other eyewear companies who were indifferent to the complaints of their sales forces.

We tried to come at it from a completely different angle. We looked at every single salesperson and if they were selling more Marchon product, they became part of the Marchon sales team; likewise, if they sold more Marcolin product. We sat down with each of them and explained what we thought were the benefits of having a second salesperson calling on their accounts. We worked hard to make them realize that the other salesperson was not the enemy. That was the sales guy or girl from one of the other companies.

This of course raised a plethora of questions—about compensation ("will I get screwed?"), sharing accounts, selecting the right division and so forth.

Choice of division was, in the end, their decision. If your sales excelled in Marcolin product, but you wanted to stay on the Marchon side, that was up to you. We encouraged them to work closely with their counterpart in the other division to share in responsibilities and information. We'd suggest exercises like taking the territory's top one-hundred accounts and dividing up primary coverage based on the ones each rep knew best. If an education program needed to be presented to a few accounts, possibly take turns doing it based on who had the strongest relationship with each. And if you learned that Dr. Jones was opening a second office, you shared that information with your counterpart in the other division. It was a system that improved efficiency and collecting account intelligence. (We also made a point of telling the reps that if there was a competitive rep in their territory that impressed them to the point where they wanted that rep on their team, we would work to make that happen.)

Then there were the money issues. It's hard to convince someone that everything will be okay when they see a chunk of their sales migrate over to someone else. The only way we figured we could resolve that issue was to give overrides for a period of time based on their partner's sales performance.

Of course there were still growing pains. We would sometimes introduce a new product line in one division and the other division would go nuts, so we had to make sure to keep it balanced when the next new line was ready to launch. It kind of forced us to develop better products for each division, and to strictly maintain that balance. We examined the basic areas of conflict and figured out how to neutralize them. And we were very good at it.

I think we completely and uniquely changed how a second sales team was launched, and it was extremely successful.

We were, in fact, so comfortable with the multi-sales team model that shortly after we introduced the first Calvin Klein collection we saw the need for a third sales organization and we went for it.

Now I can't say that some actions, like that one, weren't met with loud resentment. But we saw that resentment as valid and it fell upon us to figure out how to address it, which is the philosophy we followed with just about every decision we made. How do you take valid employee concerns or complaints and overcome them to build a better company?

In the case of the new Calvin Klein sales team we saw that if we were removing something so highly valued from a rep's portfolio, as Calvin was, we had to put something in its place. If the salesperson lost $30,000 of income by this change, one solution would be to give him or her a bonus of $30,000 for one year, along with a 1.5% override on the territory's Calvin Klein sales. Hence, at the end of the first year, the rep would be making more money than they had previously, an added expense for us, but a positive solution to a legitimate problem.

As the company matured and changed, we wound up with five separate sales divisions, and we never looked back. This was a primary driver to the explosive sales growth that made Marchon a $600 million company.

At the end of each year, we'd all inhale and exhale and go off to our national sales meeting. This was our time of renewal, to share best practices, to build *esprit de corps*, to relax, to share experiences and have fun.

The sales force would come in and they'd be tired and beat. It was like an army that had been marching for days and needed a long sleep. You could feel it; they needed to be rebuilt, to get their energy back.

The goal of our meetings was pretty consistent: to send them back into the field refreshed, excited, and raring to get back on the road with the new tools we had just furnished them. It was imperative that the meeting and what we were giving them was what they needed, not what we needed.

Crafting the meeting wasn't in itself difficult. It was a process, and as long as we put together a sales meeting that toed the line of that process we were fine. To use another metaphor, it was almost like following a rhythm, a heartbeat. If we listened to the rhythm and followed it we wouldn't create a collision (or confusion).

It was truly all in the execution; it had to be great and well-orchestrated. It was like a symphony—a slow beginning, then a rise, then a crescendo.

We covered many things in our meetings—new products, new marketing plans and advertising programs, new sales tools—but the end goal was always to reaffirm our culture and make it stronger.

Best practices was a good theme for any of our meetings. When someone hit a problem, chances were good that a lot of other people in the room at one time had had the same problem, and might have the solution. In turn, you might have a solution to a problem of theirs. We felt that this sharing was a big part of what we were as a company.

The first night we'd throw a cocktail reception, followed by dinner at their leisure. This is where Jeff really shined. He was the prince of parties and he always brought a sense of fun to these events. You could actually see people who had arrived tight as drums beginning to loosen up.

Many companies have awards presentations at their sales meetings, and we did also—to an extent. We tried to keep it very positive and not too elaborate. Obviously, if you have a couple of individuals who win all the awards then they feel great. But what about everybody else? We didn't highlight awards in our agenda.

There would certainly be an exchange of ideas, but more so a sharing of personal connections. We saw Marchon as a family and the sales meeting as the stage from which we declared it.

I would give a one-hour speech on the meeting's last day. I'd usually stay up all night prior to the speech to decide what topics to cover and in what order, but I would never write it out. This illustrated two things about my personality: 1) I'm a procrastinator; 2) I'm very hands-on. By doing the speech in the last few hours leading up to its delivery, I had the latest on what was happening.

To prepare, I had various managers sit with me the night before for about twenty or thirty minutes and give me their input. That assured that the speeches were covering the latest topics that the sales force needed to hear.

In the end I would always try to make them feel empowered and enthusiastic. "We're going out there this coming year and we're going to have a great time! Deliver a great product line and give 'em great service!"

If I did my job well I'd have them screaming and yelling and ready to go back to war.

As new influences entered the company—designer brands, new product technologies, new corporate directions—the culture of Marchon inevitably changed. But in a way it always stayed the same.

We remained a family throughout. We maintained enormous respect for each other. And even if we sometimes succumbed to "Decision Making by Argument" that was simply an expression of our passion. We all wanted the same thing: to make Marchon as successful as it could possibly be.

I believe we came close to achieving that goal by the time we sold the company in 2008. But I knew it couldn't be done without the Marchon family spirit. And so in keeping with that belief, it wasn't hard for me and Larry to agree that we should let everyone share in our financial success. So upon closing the deal we gave everyone bonuses that were announced to them through individual correspondence written in their respective languages—roughly 2,500 worldwide employees—to the tune collectively of $50 million.

CHAPTER 4

CREATING DISTINCTION THROUGH INNOVATIVE PRODUCTS

WHEN WE SET out to launch Marchon, we didn't think we were reinventing the optical industry. We basically took the playbook we had used at Avant Garde and put it to work in a new venue and under the banner of a new corporate brand.

At that time in the early 1980s, selling high-fashion European eyewear was the province of just a handful of companies (Optyl, Avant Garde and Starline, distributor of Safilo Eyewear, were the key players). Most of the product sold in the U.S. was domestically manufactured and styling was not its strong suit. The industry really hadn't changed in decades.

For that reason, retail customers (and consumers) largely viewed eyewear as a medical device product category, prosthetics for vision correction—and hence commodities, leaving the domestic suppliers with price as the only differentiator. The concept of eyewear fashion, and along with it the influence of fashion designers, was very much in its infancy, despite Europe's accelerating fashion movement.

Our first collections in those days could be characterized as well-made with European styling, though not necessarily unique. The only brands on the temples were Marcolin, which continued to distinguish itself as a top manufacturer of metal frames, and Marchon, which represented mostly acetate eyewear from other suppliers in France. Marcolin's metals production—which we had taken over from Optyl—really fueled our sales growth, representing the majority of our revenues in the first few years. Nonetheless, we recognized that if we succumbed to the attitude of "a frame is a frame," we would make our job much harder. Our job really was to break through this perception by creating products using "standard" materials, but making them very special despite this. In other words, take what exists and make it better.

Initially, our plastic product was not setting the eyewear world on fire, but it was continuously improving and it did reflect superior designs, particularly versus our domestic competitors. We were fortunate to have experienced design resources among our French manufacturing partners, and of course the Marcolin design team which provided us with so much. And we also had the benefit of important relationships at home to help guide our design and product development. Ruth White was a case in point, having the taste and knowledge to give valuable production direction to us and the European designers. From her years at Avant Garde, she had a great intuition about what worked (and what didn't) among American optical retailers and consumers.

But Marcolin was really the difference-maker for us. In Marchon's formative years, it was Marcolin product that represented the lion's share of our sales; five metal styles in particular were huge hits. With Marcolin's departure from its Optyl relationship, we realized $3 million in our first year, and much more thereafter. We agreed that we would service Optyl customers, essentially by accepting returns for a year, but that was a small investment when viewed against the revenue the Marcolin brand created.

Marcolin would prove again and again to be a valuable partner. For example, when we were preparing to launch the Calvin Klein eyewear brand, Marcolin was not only an important influence on the design; the company also helped to open doors globally (and in due course to open the door to Marchon's global expansion). Incidentally, as I mentioned earlier Giovanni's last name was not Marcolin; it was his wife's maiden name. His was Coffen. I advised him and his sons, Maurizio and Cirillo, as they were coming into a new market in the States that it might be advisable to change it. And so the family name legally became Marcolin.

One of the most important assets that Marcolin introduced to us was the young lady we met at the dawn of the relationship, Giancarla Agnoli. Starting as our liaison to the company, Giancarla became involved in every aspect of our business—from product development to sales, marketing and most definitely distribution. She quickly proved invaluable to Marchon and finally became the head of our Marchon Italy operation, which incorporated our headquarters and distribution facilities, an R&D center and production initiatives.

Giancarla was just one component of the support Marcolin gave us as we expanded internationally. As they had already opened distribution in countries outside of Italy, Marchon was able to capitalize on their experience and their knowledge of these foreign markets.

Eventually, and in retrospect it was probably inevitable, Marchon and Marcolin had become these two very big and somewhat unwieldy companies. Additionally our product strategies were beginning to diverge. So in 1997, our two companies decided to part ways. We were committed to making sure that the transition took place without a ripple, assisting them in finding a new headquarters, a U.S. management team and even providing the dedicated second sales force that was selling Marcolin product for us.

For our part, we had the good fortune to hire Giancarla, although it was not a quid pro quo. She had spent so many years in service to Marchon that it seemed only natural for her to officially join our team.

We had also come to recognize that the eyewear made by Marcolin and our other European suppliers, while excellent in quality, did not do much to distinguish Marchon from its many U.S. competitors in the view of most eye care professionals. Those were the days when the industry was dominated by "house" brands, as opposed to more consumer-oriented designer or fashion brands. While every company was touting the uniqueness of its product's styling, coloration and fit (none more so than Marchon), the average eye care professional could purchase either Product X or Product Y and not really make a mistake. This was made even more true by the very lax return policies most companies had adopted.

I knew that we needed to offer product that featured a great "Wow!" factor, the likes of which the buyer had not seen before. We depended on our sales force to be our eyes and ears and report back anything happening in the field that was noteworthy.

In 1986, we began to get reports about a new polymer being used to produce eyewear called carbon fiber graphite (CFG).

The material had already been applied in the aerospace and automotive industries due to its strength, durability and lightness—qualities that made it equally attractive for eyewear. It's also highly flexible and easier to work with than more brittle materials.

After some research we determined that the best suppliers of carbon fiber frames were based in Japan. We soon connected with a manufacturer's rep named Terry Makara, who assisted in putting together a deal for exclusive distribution with a factory called Takeda. It was imperative for us to have an exclusive relationship with the supplier for a number of reasons—competitive advantage, product consistency and quality control, and the manufacturer's proprietary patented formulation (which I believed was better than other carbon fiber products on the market).

Marchon was in a unique position in that our not being dominated by a single factory allowed us the freedom to source unique products from a variety of manufacturers around the world.

For CFG, we only used one supplier and we always maintained a fair financial relationship, which is how we dealt with all our vendors. I was always less interested in what the product cost and more concerned with how the product sold, and sold through.

We planned to call the collection CFG, for obvious reasons. It was phenomenal eyewear. Not only was it lightweight and strong, we could make it in an array of amazing, vibrant colors. We applied basic styles—like the conservative, vintage P-3 shape—and added spring hinges. We were also able to keep the suggested retail price under $100.

CFG went gangbusters, adding rocket fuel to our sales engine. Our customers could immediately see that a product that was lightweight, durable, yet still colorful and fashionable, was an undisputed winner. Within a short period of time following its release, CFG was selling at the rate of 20,000 units per month. By the early 1990s, we had sold over one million pairs.

During its rollout, we came up with a unique counter card that we called the CFG "Magic Window." It was basically a picture of various eyewear styles in black and white, but when you raised the image via a cardboard tab so that it appeared in the "window" the frames came to life and displayed their many diverse, exciting colors. The concept was such a popular vehicle to illustrate one of CFG's unique features that we also had it inserted into one of the leading industry magazines, *20/20*, where it received still more attention.

In a short time, and despite there being other competitors in carbon fiber eyewear, Marchon became virtually synonymous with the category and it garnered us much attention. CFG opened doors for us.

The meteoric success of CFG taught me a few things: that unique technology in eyewear manufacturing had the potential to create an immediate, competitive distinction; that exclusivity and control of the patents for such products were vital; and that the sales team had to be well-versed in how to "tell the story".

But if the CFG sensation made Marchon a premier industry brand in the U.S., what followed that introduction a year later was literally the first step in Marchon's ascendance to the world stage.

I had traveled to Montreal to visit Nonu Ifergan, the owner of a company called Aspex Eyewear. Nonu was distributing the CFG product in the Canadian market and I was interested in learning more about his company and comparing notes on the CFG launch.

When I arrived, Nonu was in the middle of another meeting with Eiichi Nakanishi, the founder of Nakanishi Optical, an eyewear manufacturer based in Osaka, Japan. They were intently examining a metal eyeglass frame as if it were a rare gem.

Nonu was always fascinated by new technologies that could potentially change the eyewear marketplace. I fell in love with the frame immediately; it was very light and durable, a perfect men's frame.

"Look at this," Nonu said, as he bent the eyeglass temple to a ninety degree angle. Remarkably, the temple returned to its original shape. I knew in that instant that Marchon had to have that frame. It seemed to offer everything a perfect eyeglass needs—a superior men's metal product.

The history of memory metal, and in particular memory metal eyewear, is a long one, peppered with many apocryphal anecdotes.

The original metal alloy was called NiTinol (Nickel Titanium Naval Ordnance Labs) and it was discovered in 1961 very much by accident by William Buehler, a metallurgist working for the Navy to develop a material for rockets that could withstand the high temperatures when returning to earth's atmosphere.

While testing the material, Buehler bent and twisted it out of shape to determine its strength and pliability. On his way out to lunch, he left the sample material on a window sill in direct sunlight. When he returned he was amazed to see that the sample was back to its original shape.

Memory metal was a metal looking for an application and several were found, most notably for medical devices. The one impediment to its obtaining widespread use was the heat requirement to bring it back to its original form.

For a number of years, NiTinol had vanished from the market (some conspiracy theorists believed the government had withdrawn it because the material was actually top secret, a remnant of the crashed alien spacecraft in Roswell, N.M.).

In the early 1980s, an executive with the Boston Consulting Group, Bob Zider, happened upon NiTinol and saw immediate possibilities. He started the Beta Group, a business dedicated to bringing new inventions to market, in partnership with Boston Consulting and set to work on applications for the memory metal. He soon came upon eyewear as a logical use. Being an eyeglasses wearer himself, he knew how easily eyewear could become broken or misshapen.

Zider took the new material, along with his eyewear patents, to Nakanishi Optical where the prototype product was developed. Zider returned to the U.S. with his memory metal eyewear, which still required heat to activate the memory. He also purchased a New England eyewear distributor called Universal Optical, and set about introducing memory metal eyewear to America.

The eyeglass frame that Nonu showed me was based on a second-generation formulation that Nakanishi had come up with, which would return to shape at room temperature.

We immediately made arrangements with Nakanishi to bring his memory metal product to the U.S. Nakanishi had a relationship with a competing U.S. distributor, Tura, as well as a German company with an American presence called Neostyle, and they each had placed a few orders although they weren't actually on the market yet. But Nakanishi felt he wanted to honor the orders.

It didn't make sense to me to have both Marchon and these other companies selling memory metal eyewear, so I told Nakanishi that if we were to go forward I'd like him to consider giving Marchon exclusivity, and we in turn would work with him exclusively and build a big production capacity.

We started with a product line we called Autoflex, positioned as a sub-collection of Marchon for the Marchon sales force. Once again, we trained the sales team to train the customers about how the product worked, its fundamental features and why it made a good choice for their patients.

Autoflex was a hit right out of the box. I would have been surprised if the market reaction was anything but "Wow!"

It was easy to see that there would soon be competitors running around trying to sell an inferior memory metal product. But we made it quite clear that if a practitioner wanted to carry Autoflex he'd have to present it in a very precise way that emphasized that not all memory metals were the same. Of course, we anticipated that practitioners would have problems presenting and differentiating the product, so we impressed upon them that they needed to be consistent and by no means break on price.

Bob Zider was certainly still out there with his first-generation memory metal product that still required heat to regain its shape, and he had his distribution company, Universal Optical, which apparently had not performed well. But Bob also had his patents.

Bob claimed that his patents also covered our products, a claim we initially disputed. Over time, we realized that he had a valid claim, and rather than spend more time and money on countering him we did the smart thing and bought him out.

Now Marchon had the patents exclusively and we had an exclusive relationship with Nakanishi for the production. We had everything under one roof.

We also obtained another valuable advantage in our engagement with Bob Zider, and that was an introduction to David Chute. Dave was a colleague of Bob's from both the Boston Consulting Group and the Beta Group, who had developed a keen interest in the memory metal eyewear category, and through a licensing agreement with Zider, was in the process of starting his own frames company called Flex Eyewear using Bob's original formulation.

When we met Dave we immediately liked him. He was a very sharp marketer and had an innate aptitude for the eyewear space. His Flex Eyewear was generating about $1 million per year within a short time. We bought the business, and convinced Dave to come to Marchon and head up the memory metal introduction for us.

Autoflex continued to be a huge hit for the Marchon division, much to the Marcolin division's chagrin. So Dave came up with a solution by introducing a product for the Marcolin folks called Accuflex (the first-generation product from Flex Eyewear), which we positioned as a higher-end frame (think BMW versus Chevrolet). Accuflex frames initially had electroplated, flat temples with soldered hinges. Autoflex had silver, rounded temples without the soldered hinges.

Accuflex was also crucial to our ability to expand memory metal's customer base. Where we were initially only thinking in terms of the men's market, we were able to raise the styling on Accuflex to a higher fashion level which would appeal to women as well as more fashion-conscious men.

Now we had memory metal products that appealed to the average Joes who appreciated the utility of Autoflex and the fashionistas who were attracted to the more upscale Accuflex. We also had a way to keep both sales teams happy by complementing each other rather than competing.

Dave also helped us brand and market the memory eyewear material as Flexon. His thinking was that like materials such as Gore-Tex and Teflon, the Flexon brand would represent a superior eyewear product that offered a superior wearing experience. (Dave would soon become a highly valued executive vice president with Marchon, growing beyond memory metal to take charge of many different areas of the operation, including the introductions of the Nike brand and Airlock, our incredibly successful three-piece mounting system.)

Patents obviously don't last forever, but we put together a strategic plan that allowed us to have a very solid business even after the patents expired. We made it clear through our marketing that Flexon was one of a kind; it could be imitated but never duplicated. And of course competitors would eventually try to enter the flexible eyewear market, but they faced two hurdles: our patents were still in force, and their formulations were inferior.

When the patents did finally expire we took the high road. We had a superior product in materials, production and design, and we pointed to our twenty-plus years of achievement and our over twenty-two million satisfied wearers, primarily in the U.S. and Canada. We knew we had made it when a 1993 cover of *Rolling Stone* magazine featured late night host David Letterman, wearing Flexon.

Memory metal eyewear was so popular that several optical chain retailers wanted to get into the category with their own products. While we didn't sell to them as a rule, remaining dedicated to our core market of independent practitioners, we frequently convinced them that a private-label version of Flexon was the better option.

Walmart Optical, for example, was eager to bring out their own flexible eyewear to be called Bendables. We offered them a private label program and they went for it, with great success. (That was the first time we sold Walmart anything.) Eventually, when they were no longer encumbered by our patents, they developed their own product but soon discovered that their formulation and manufacturing quality couldn't match ours.

Other chain retailers were still after Flexon, recognizing the strong franchise the brand had already established among independent outlets. In truth, the business was too lucrative for us to turn down, but we set up some ground rules. First, they were not to discount the product under any circumstances. Second, they had to maintain the brand's integrity and be willing to promote Flexon as opposed to some house brand. With the exception of a few regional players that Dave had managed to engage, the only national chain to take us up on the offer was Lenscrafters. The Lenscrafters connection catapulted Flexon to heights we never imagined.

Shortly after, Dave came up with the idea of creating a cable television ad campaign with Lenscrafters to promote Flexon on a nationwide basis. He had done some limited-reach campaigns with the regional retailers he was working with and achieved some nice results. I was admittedly dubious; no one had ever advertised eyewear to consumers on television before, and a TV campaign was sure to be a big investment. Dave provided some comfort in telling me that the $3 million campaign would be funded equally by Marchon and Lenscrafters (they considered our $1.5 million as co-op money).

The campaign ran for six weeks in 1995 in spots appearing on the History Channel, CNN, Comedy Central and a number of other popular networks. It represented several firsts in eyewear advertising, not the least of which was that it was the first time Lenscrafters advertised a specific product, as opposed to the quality of their optometrists or one-hour service.

By the end of those six weeks, we went from selling 40,000 units of Flexon per month to 80,000 units, and never declined.

In a relatively short time, Flexon was generating over $100 million in sales annually, representing 15%-20% of our overall revenue. To handle that level of production and to keep costs down, Marchon and Nakanishi created a joint venture in China to open a memory metals factory, which is now called NiTec Eyewear.

Eventually, Flexon became so explosive that it found its way into a number of Marchon's premier branded collections, such as Nike, Nautica and Calvin Klein. (Nike, by the way, had never licensed their brand to any other company, but did so with us—after eighteen months of negotiation—because we were able to co-brand Nike Vision with Flexon.)

The introduction of Flexon capped the formative first five years of Marchon's evolution. The company was now on a very solid footing. It also began a new chapter of tremendous growth, major changes and equally major challenges.

CHAPTER 5

GETTING CLOSER TO
THE CUSTOMER BY
REDEFINING SERVICE

WE WERE VERY lucky that from the outset we served a very different customer base than most of our competitors (with a few notable exceptions).

When Marchon first opened its doors, the majority of eyewear suppliers/manufacturers were selling to wholesale distributors who would in turn sell those goods to their customers, the eye care professionals. While selling had been done this way in the U.S. for decades there were some very obvious flaws with this method.

For one thing, the wholesalers' sales teams were selling many brands from many companies, not just one. Every supplier who followed this model was vying for the same wholesale customer, resulting in a sales sample case full of many frames from many different factories. While the suppliers would frequently create incentive programs to get the reps to show their products first, there was no guarantee that they would. Plus there were so many incentive programs out there that there was little differentiation.

Secondly, unless they worked for a stock house, the reps had much more to sell than frames. Their first priority was to sell laboratory services to the retailer or practitioner. For the most part, producing eyeglass Rx lenses was the wholesaler's reason to be. On top of that, many wholesalers' reps were also selling tools, equipment and accessories. That sales bag had become awfully big and awfully full.

With regard to frames, the rep would frequently take the path of least resistance—if the practitioner had a particular fondness for frames from Brand X, that's what the rep would show. Hence, a new style or collection would really have to fight its way out of the bag in order to get noticed. And even if by some miracle that occurred, the reps would frequently be ill-equipped to talk about its features and benefits.

For a handful of suppliers like us (most notably Avant Garde, Starline, Optyl and a few others, including another new, start up company called Viva Optique) the sales model was completely different. We bypassed the wholesaler's rep and recruited sales people to call directly on the practitioner.

This approach addressed many of the shortcomings of the "two-step" sales model: our people only had one thing to sell (well, two things in both Marchon and Marcolin) and they were instructed on how to talk about the product and ways in which we'd give it marketing support through in-store merchandising and advertising. The rep would also be able to assist the buyer in displaying the product and would be able to respond to any complaints, etc., that the buyer might have.

In the old model, the buyer or customer was surrounded by so much "bubble wrap" that a connection with the manufacturer couldn't be made.

The old model suppliers did inevitably cultivate another important customer group, the multi-location practices and chain store operations which very quickly represented a larger and larger share of their total sales (at risk to their profit margins). But for many, that was their salvation and it remains so to this day.

Selling direct, as it came to be known, was all that we knew from our Avant Garde days, and for that we were fortunate. (The establishment companies, however, looked at us as pariahs and would not include us in the steering of the industry, to the extent that they could keep us out.)

At that time in the mid-1980s, the optical market was being transformed by influences both within and without. Retailing in general was becoming more specialized and more dynamic than ever before—the era of "one store fits all" was rapidly coming to an end. And optical was suddenly catching up.

Up to that point, the optical practitioner was something of an authoritarian "gatekeeper," who selected the frames he or she wanted you to choose from, sent them off to the optical lab and vaguely promised to have them ready for you in about two weeks.

But all that changed, by my reckoning, shortly after we launched Marchon, for several reasons: 1) fashion was truly beginning to inform the eyewear category, and smart practitioners realized that they would have to get with the program or be left out; and 2) a new optical retail concept—Lenscrafters' promise of glasses in an hour—captured the consumer's imagination. The average eyewear customer had never experienced that level of service before, and when coupled with the vast selection of frame styles that Lenscrafters offered, altered the original practitioner/patient dynamic forever.

In many ways, it was a great time to start an eyewear company, especially as we came at it with no prejudices. Recognizing that top customer service was proliferating at the retail level alerted us to the need for flawless customer service at the wholesale level. To us it just made sense; if the product can help you stand out just so far, then the service component of delivering and supporting the product must be stellar. We were dedicated to creating the best eyewear company, highlighted by the best buyer experience that the optical industry had ever known.

There was a keen focus on service within the company that was really without peer in the industry. We had this army in the field, eventually three-hundred-plus sales reps, which was our direct connection, or touch-point, to the customer. Complementing the reps was the internal customer service team, our second touch-point.

You start with a vision to be the best supplier to the customer. In order to achieve this you have to have the best service possible, the best systems possible, the best information possible and, of course, the best people possible.

Not only did we need the best people, but we needed them to become true business partners with each of their customers—providing an array of services from education to marketing to industry intelligence. As eyewear became more fashionable thanks to the growing influence of European suppliers, it became a more important product category to the retail customer. And with that growth in importance, the customer needed many more services and much more engagement with the supplier.

We had to know at all times what the customer needed and respond to it immediately. Again, this is where the sales rep becomes the customer's best advocate, and also in effect another level of "customer" to us.

It was our steadfast objective to maintain price integrity at all times, regardless of the customer. That's not to say that we didn't provide discounts for high-volume purchases or buys made through the buying groups (of which I was not particularly fond). But we didn't want the reps haggling with each single-location practitioner over a handful of frames.

So we presented the case to customers that instead of discounting, we were investing more money in marketing, education, service, staff training and a number of other things to make the independent practice thrive.

Remember, as the Lenscrafters revolution shook our world at the supplier level, it did far more shaking of the independent practitioner who was ill-equipped to compete in this arena. We offered to give them the tools to do so—if they became Marchon customers. This was a strategy that none of our U.S. competitors were applying and it became a significant point of distinction for us.

However, it wasn't by any means easy to execute or, for that matter, to convince practitioners that they needed it.

Our success was directly tied to their success, so it was essential for us to help them understand how our products were unique and produced better profits than cheaper products that they viewed as commodities.

From a typical practitioner's perspective, if we offered a product at $50 wholesale and he or she could get a different frame at $30 wholesale and the retail price for either could be about the same, then the profit margin generated by the $30 frame would be greater. We had to show them that the two products were not the same and had to assist them in delivering that message to the consumer, because we knew that the consumer would understand the differences. Good product quality meant happier patients, and that meant higher patient retention rates and more referrals.

I can't emphasize enough how the "secret sauce" in this formula was a well-trained and committed sales force, supported by an equally well-trained and committed customer service department.

In many ways, it was a continuous cycle that built upon itself. Knowing what the customer wanted and providing it through the touch-point of the sales rep was critical to growth for everyone involved. It improved the practitioner's business, helped the rep succeed and fueled Marchon's rapid rise.

But while the sales rep was a vital touch-point, the customer service rep was in many ways more involved. A customer might call in orders two or three times per week, so that CSR had to always be on top of it.

We had a hard-and-fast rule that if an order came in prior to 3pm, it would ship that day. We made sure of it through our delivery systems (this is where Jeff would come in and build that foolproof system), and through the CSR, who would go down to shipping to make sure that everything went out as promised.

As we got bigger and bigger it became harder to execute that—but we did. There are many who believe that perfection is not realistic, that failure is an inevitable fact of business life, but I disagree. If you conduct fifty transactions in a row and execute them perfectly, but then screw up on the fifty-first, to our way of thinking that was not acceptable—if the rule is that everything has to be perfect, then that one failure is glaring. We would not tolerate that failure. But if 99%

of my competition thinks that perfection is not realistic, that the one failure is tolerable, then that's the best result, in my opinion, for me and Marchon.

Did we experience problematic customers or failed transactions? Admittedly, we did. But we addressed them immediately, by first putting out the fire. If it's a case where the consumer's blaming the doctor and the doctor is blaming us, then we'd call the consumer personally and vow to make it better. We would then make sure to learn from the problem and create new systems, or fine-tune existing systems to make sure it didn't happen again.

Sometimes we'd also lose a customer, although I'm proud to say it was atypical. If a customer was ready to fire us, we'd obviously start by determining the problem. We'd also try to understand if the customer's complaints were right—or wrong. This would give us some insight into what the customer was about.

Regardless of where the blame laid, we tried to figure out how we could save the customer. Candidly, there were times when it was almost impossible, and times when the customer, in fact, should have been "fired". That didn't happen a lot but when it did it upset us.

Others might say "I won't waste my time on this guy," and just go after other customers. Our philosophy was that you don't move on, you don't walk away from the customer if you can help it. There was a saying at Proctor & Gamble that, in effect, one customer complaint can be like 10,000. You may have lost that one customer for life, but if he talks to other customers you could potentially lose many more. People don't forget. So if you don't put the fire out it can spread, and spread rapidly.

I was very proud of the reputation we had established as industry leaders in customer service. In fact, the trade magazine, *20/20*, featured an annual survey of their readership to find out who excelled in the various quality categories for an eyewear company and Marchon always came out on top in the category of customer service.

At one point about five years after we launched, we experienced a customer service "hiccup," when our original CS manager left the company. Within a week's time we were falling behind on orders and getting materials to the reps much later than we should.

Our immediate priority was obviously finding a great candidate for the manager's spot, and to our great fortune it didn't take us long. In March of 1988, Deb Ingino walked into the Marchon conference room and just amazed us.

"Tell me something," I remember asking her, "where does customer service begin and where does it end?"

Her eyes lit up and she became incredibly animated. "Everything about the business is customer service!" she said.

She then explained that it started at the receptionist's desk, made its rounds of every other department and it didn't end until the customer was opening the package. And while customer service is not directly involved in many of those processes, it strongly influences them by the culture it helps create.

"Customer service is paramount," she said, emphatically. "And you have to do it perfectly."

I was floored! "Damn, that's good," was all I could say.

Deb joined us immediately thereafter, and I must say that she practiced what she preached. She had an entrepreneur's heart and took ownership of the position to create new systems and protocols that helped us get back on track. It took us close to sixty days to get everything right again, but it was clear the customers were on our side—they were actually excited that we were returning to our old form.

We also had to rectify the service issues with our other customer base, the sales team. The CS team recognized that we had to be committed to making our reps look like problem-solvers, business advisors and partners to the customer. In short, we had to make them look terrific.

In order to do this, we gathered our team together and created a subordinate department called Sales Rep Service, dedicated to nothing more than supplying the reps with necessary materials, responding to their requests, and simply helping them succeed.

Deb went on to play a significant role in our global expansion, but more on that later.

As our customer service philosophy evolved, we realized that we weren't simply selling eyewear to retail customers—essentially anyone could do that. We were providing a fairly comprehensive suite of services to assist in making our customers better—merchandising and marketing, education, and sales training, among other items. Again, our belief was that there was more value in these various services and an ongoing, beneficial customer/supplier relationship than another 10% off the wholesale price of the product. Luckily, the average Marchon customer came to believe that too.

We also determined that there were many different ways to identify and define service. We wanted our customers to view Marchon as a true business solution, providing access to the tools and resources to succeed in an ever-changing, highly competitive environment.

With that objective in mind, I began researching other categories within the optical marketplace whose products or services complemented what we did. In a short time, I came upon a Pennsylvania-based optical display and retail space design company called Eye Designs, LLC, which was founded and operated by the Winig family. In 1996, we acquired a 50% interest in their company and began to capitalize on the display business. Not only did this provide us with a new revenue stream and a logical extension of our service mission, it also gave us another vehicle to promote the Marchon brand (all their catalog prototypes of displays and practice remodels featured visuals of Marchon eyewear).

We also determined that, after twenty years of catering pretty much exclusively to independent eyecare practitioners, we'd broaden our customer base to include multi-location corporate retail businesses. But we knew that we'd have to create a new service paradigm in order to execute properly. So in 2003, we started a subsidiary company, based in New York City, which we called Allure Eyewear. Allure's array of services included many that were designed strictly to accommodate these big retail customers, such as unique eyewear brands and an extensive private label program (it was always my conviction that big retail wasn't interested in buying "house" brands from us, as they could simply go to the overseas factories and source the product on their own; the Allure private label program satisfied that need).

Additionally, as with our independent customer base, we provided more extensive education and training to our larger retailers, in lieu of falling into the discounting trap. We simply took what worked at the single-location level and scaled it up for the bigger buyers.

But to my mind, one of the most important moves we made to expand our service contributions was to get into the practice management software business through the acquisition of a West Coast-based firm called OfficeMate.

We had learned that Luxottica was in the process of introducing a practice management software product that they were calling EZ Frame. (The basic structure of their software, we were led to believe, was derived from a dental practice management program being marketed by Henry Schein, Inc., a global supplier of medical products.)

To my way of thinking, software management systems were consistent with Marchon's service objectives, and with that in mind (and in order to keep Luxottica from getting the upper hand), I determined that we needed to pursue this category in response. I felt it was imperative to keep an eye on Luxottica because I believed very strongly that they could provide a roadmap to Marchon's future.

So in the fall of 1994, we entered the software business with OfficeMate, which was managed by its original co-developer and president, Ed Buffington, and his partner and co-developer, Stephen Rosenbaum. At the time, computerization was exploding in just about every profession and we felt confident that it would become a staple of the optometrist's office as we went forward.

Ed had introduced what you might call the "Quicken Business Model" to the OfficeMate proposition, meaning that he would charge an annual licensing fee (as opposed to a prohibitive one-time sale price), and continue to provide software updates. Eventually, at around the time we purchased the company, OfficeMate converted over to a one-time license fee of $695 for single users and $895 for multi-users.

Apparently, there was concern among some of the customer base that an annual fee might have a tendency to increase every year.

OfficeMate proved to be an invaluable tool for the vision care practice of the 1990s and beyond. The software could provide solutions for inventory management, patient recall, filing insurance claims, billing and payables, and eventually electronic medical records.

With just 1,900 users and revenues of about $2 million at the time we acquired them, we knew that we would have to make a more extensive investment to get OfficeMate to where we thought it should be. We immediately put together an ad campaign to address many of the concerns a practitioner might have about entering the computer age: ease of use, organization of records and cost. OfficeMate had answers for all of it.

We also invested in a new 20 ft. by 20 ft. trade show booth for them and readily integrated their culture with ours (over the years, while we maintained a somewhat "hands off" approach to managing OfficeMate, we probably invested another $10 million-$15 million in the business).

But the investment clearly paid off; by the time Marchon was sold in 2008, OfficeMate had over 10,000 users, was generating about $18 million annually, and became the largest-selling software solution in the vision care field—a growth spurt that the previous owners admitted would not have happened without Marchon's resources. Also, the company that purchased all of the Marchon assets, Vision Service Plan (VSP), viewed OfficeMate as the missing piece in their own digital puzzle, pairing the capabilities of their online claims portal with the information-gathering software product.

The moves to expand beyond just the eyewear space through the acquisitions of Eye Designs and OfficeMate put Marchon in a league all its own when it came to customer service, a fact we touted highly in our advertising, informing the marketplace that we could provide them with the "Turnkey Office."

CHAPTER 6

MARKETING MAGIC— LOOK BIG (EVEN WHEN YOU'RE SMALL)

AS WE WERE preparing to launch Marchon, we talked a lot about how we wanted the brand to be perceived among prospective accounts. Though ours was a new business, we brought to it a wealth of experience and the expertise we drew from having managed one of the industry's most prominent and successful eyewear companies, Avant Garde.

How did we want the vision community to view Marchon? As creative, energetic or proficient? Yes to all of those descriptions. But mostly we wanted prospective accounts (along with salespeople and competitors) to see Marchon as substantial, powerful, big—even when we weren't—and a legitimate competitor to the company we left behind.

From Day One, we wanted the optical world to know that we were dedicated to building one of the biggest eyewear companies in the market.

This is where our marketing initiatives came in. As we formulated our plans, we always had a vision of what the outcome should be, what the message we were hoping to convey was. As they emerged over the years from a medical device mentality, it seemed that a number of eyewear companies didn't apply that kind of critical thinking to their marketing and advertising. It appeared that a number of our competitors were driven by their egos. They had to have the biggest trade show booths and the most advertising pages in the industry magazines.

Marketing was an extension of the Marchon personality, and more than any individual product or collection or licensed brand, maintaining that personality was clearly the foremost objective. When it came to B2B marketing, we wanted to deliver a message to our accounts and our sales people that they made the right choice in choosing Marchon.

Initially, we did that by playing to our strengths—the expertise we built at Avant Garde, the partnership with Marcolin (we ran a trade ad when we first started that trumpeted the partnership with the headline, "Together Again for the First Time," implying that our and Marcolin's industry know-how made us partners, in effect, before we were actually partners).

We also inundated the trade magazines with ad spreads, a large but still relatively conservative investment that positioned us in the collective industry imagination as being at the top of the heap—a fabulous ROI.

As we made our presence felt more and more in the marketplace, we always tried to do things with our trade marketing that broke through the clutter and were memorable. And the best way to be memorable was to interact with the customer.

We were very fortunate to come across a novelty item that we called Fuzzies (they were actually called Weepuls)—little, round, fuzzy toy figures with flowing, bright red hair, antennae and big, silver eyeglasses. The round shape and red hair we thought would be reminiscent of the red "O" in the Marchon logo, making it even more memorable.

I called them Marchon Martians and we introduced them at our first official sales meeting in a pretty unique way.

One night during the meeting, while the reps were finishing their dinner, the lights in the ballroom went dark and weird music and unusual sounds followed. Dry ice was used to create smoke which was infused with blue lights from above.

As the hotel staff wheeled in hundreds of 12-inch diameter red

Fuzzies stacked on dish carts, I was hidden behind a curtain and began to do my best Orson Wells impression from "War of the Worlds". I then told the story of the Marchon Martians taking over the optical world. The reps loved it and within several minutes all the Fuzzies were gone.

After that introduction, we supplied the reps with half-inch versions of the Fuzzies to give out to accounts. We also handed out tons of them at trade shows and ordered about 10,000 of these smaller Fuzzies each year. The smaller Fuzzies had adhesive on the bottoms of their feet so that our accounts could affix them to computers, phone receivers and mirrors.

When the company was sold, the new ownership decided to discontinue the Fuzzies, but they had made their mark on the optical industry. Years afterward, reps would tell of seeing them in practices throughout the U.S. I considered that a big win for Marchon customer interaction.

One of my favorite ad campaigns from our early days was called the Marchon "Hot Copy" Contest, created by our ad agency at the time, Arthur Kramer Advertising, with our input. The premise was to get accounts to submit a tagline for Marchon's ads, the winner receiving the phenomenal prize of a Mercedes Benz. That bit of marketing audaciousness was unheard of in the optical industry. The winner, a lady who became a Marchon customer after participating in the contest, opted instead to take a cash prize of $25,000. Her submission, which we used in our ad materials afterward, was "Tomorrow's Success Begins with Marchon Today," a perfect rendering of the Marchon persona.

Based on that success, we held a "scratch and win" contest to showcase Flexon several years later, the prize for both the eye care professional and consumer being a Mini-Cooper.

And there was the CFG retail counter card we called "The Magic Window," which dramatically highlighted the wide range of vivid colors in the collection. The mechanism was actually quite simple, but it captured the imagination of the entire marketplace and it accelerated the popularity of CFG quite dramatically.

I was very drawn to ideas and marketing projects that were fun and different, a little bit sexy but also capable of generating the broadest appeal. It's funny. Donna Rollins and the Marchon creative team would bring me a host of ideas and those that got rejected went into the Marchon "Graveyard," from where they might be resurrected later on and then approved. Candidly, when these ideas would emerge—as was the case with "The Magic Window"—I'd throw caution to the wind and spend whatever it took to make them happen.

We loved to conjure up the "Wow!" factor, impressing the industry with our innovation and our intuitive sense of what motivated accounts. Our tradeshow exhibit booths, for example, were meticulously designed by Gilbert Displays to be inviting environments. There was only one entrance so that guests could be greeted properly. We wanted to make people feel comfortable, like they were in our living room, with every detail carefully thought out, and all of them sending very subtle visual cues to the accounts.

For example, we'd feature bowls of M&M's to remind visitors of the partnership between Marchon & Marcolin. And we had vases of red roses at the booth throughout the show, because the visual image of a rose in bloom was reminiscent of the red "O" in the Marchon logo (we gave away the roses at the end of each show, and for many attending it was a memorable event). We also hung an American Flag in the booth, indicating we believed that while we stood among the other world-class international eyewear companies, we were uniquely American and did business in an American fashion.

There was no sales pressure; we wanted people to come in and browse, but over a three-day period we'd write $1-$2 million in orders.

And then there were the West Coast tradeshow parties! Admittedly, in this instance we didn't set out to create an iconic marketing vehicle, but that's what we ended up with. Our sales in the West were particularly strong thanks to the efforts of Barry and Nina Lerner, our transplants from Florida who had migrated to California and dominated the West Coast markets.

We were in the midst of introducing the Bob Mackie license for eyewear, and the western show at that time—called Vision Expo—was in Anaheim, CA.

"You know, it's really boring in Anaheim at night…even Disney is closed," Nina told me, Larry and Jeff during a conference call. "We should have our own party, like a casino night."

It didn't take much convincing on Nina's part. We decided to feature a casino in one room, a disco in the other and celebrate the launch of Bob Mackie with a fashion show. Also, we opened the party up to everyone—doctors, staff, even competitors. The first party was so successful that we made it an annual tradition, and remarkably wound up with 5,000 people attending, literally emptying out the three major trade show hotels there.

Again, the feeling was that you could go big without having to mortgage the company. Rather than hire a party planner and service to put on the event, we negotiated with the Anaheim Marriott for the space and our people did the work. We'd have our sales reps at the entrances to assist the attendees and offer guests a couple of drink tickets and a little food. The early Anaheim parties cost under $100,000 to host.

Eventually, the parties became so big that they were a bear to manage, and our salespeople complained about the throngs of attendees at every entrance clamoring to get in. "How does Disney manage the crowds?" I asked them. So we came up with a very simple system for admitting our impatient guests. During the show that day, the attendee would have to pick up a wristband at our booth in order to get into the party. In that way, we assured an easy access for the guest *and* we gave them yet another reason to stop by our booth.

When the West Coast show moved to Las Vegas, the Marchon party moved with it. At that point, the party had become part of Marchon's identity. We took a twenty-one-acre venue at the Flamingo Hilton, and the party continued to grow to the point where it became a city-wide event, according to the Flamingo's management. To get those kinds of crowds in what amounts to America's biggest playground was, I think, testimony to the power of the Marchon brand and reputation.

Of course, we couldn't keep the cost below $100,000 in Las Vegas, but the Flamingo was so pleased with all the additional traffic their hotel received that they wound up giving us the space at no charge for as long as we were there. Regardless, we were spending just under $250,000 but we always felt that the return on investment was very high.

Much of our marketing had a more practical purpose but still served the same objectives. In particular, I'm thinking of our educational programs that, at the time, were easily the most comprehensive in the industry. I always considered marketing and education to be linked; both are brand-builders and both leave the customer more informed.

Education, we believed, provided us with several competitive advantages and our accounts with added value. As we were not price-cutters, the educational programs gave us a way to reward accounts that avoided the issue of deeper discounts. In fact, we set it up so that accounts could apply a portion of their marketing co-op dollars to education for themselves and their staff.

Our other advantage was inherent in the educational content. We emphasized topics that were designed to help practitioners increase revenue, train their staff and attract more clients, in effect making them better accounts for Marchon. It wasn't very difficult to assemble these educational programs. We'd literally get our best salespeople together and "download" their brains to extract the tips and recommendations on best management and marketing practices they'd seen working in the field, and our "inside" group, under Donna Rollins' direction, would work with this information to create good, topical educational and training content.

We also hired on a very prominent optometrist, Dr. Jack Weber, to help in crafting our education in a peer-to-peer format. For the doctors it was primarily about operating the business effectively, but for the staff which was involved with the actual sale, it was all about the product, how it should be presented and merchandised, and how to maintain a revenue focus.

Eventually, it became necessary to launch a full education department, and we did so with the help of Fred Humphrey, our twenty-fifth hire.

Fred had some optical experience, but the bulk of his career was spent in the recording industry, working for CBS. Regardless, he had the creative capacity to develop courses, for both live presentations and home study, and the organizational skill to train our salespeople (with help from our "inside" team) to also be good educators and service the entire customer base. Collectively, we supplied the best materials we could develop to the sales team so they could readily understand the message and make expert presentations. (Fred would later play a major role in Marchon's global expansion.)

When our B2B marketing was progressing effectively, we began to turn our attention to the eyewear consumer. For the most part, throughout optical's long history, consumer advertising and PR played at most a small role in the marketing of eyewear. The eye care practitioners (primarily opticians and optometrists) were the gatekeepers of eyewear products and pretty much controlled the whole purchasing process, with the patient (a.k.a., the consumer) blithely following along. But that was beginning to change.

Many companies, particularly technology-driven operations, were innovating dramatically. In the late 1980s, for example, Johnson & Johnson introduced the first disposable soft contact lens—a major breakthrough in consumer convenience. Knowing that they had to broadcast that message, the company launched an extensive consumer advertising and awareness campaign. The result was a highly successful product that dominates its market to this day.

Not long after that event, a company that was born out of a joint venture between PPG Industries, makers of optical monomers and coatings, among other things, and ophthalmic lens giant Essilor, opened its doors in Florida to create the first ever photochromatic, lightweight plastic lenses (lenses that change from clear to dark in sunlight). The company and the product were called Transitions. Like J&J, the execs running Transitions knew that their product message had to proliferate among the eyewear purchasing public, and decided to spend tens of millions—unprecedented amounts for the optical category—on widespread consumer advertising and marketing.

As I discussed previously, when the opportunity to advertise Flexon in consumer media arose, I'll be honest and say that I was reluctant at first. Television, which was what we were considering as the cornerstone of our program, was certainly not cheap. But I gave consideration to two things: Flexon was a unique product for both eye care professionals and their patients, and while we enjoyed exclusivity in the memory metal space at the time, that wouldn't last forever. There are many patents on Flexon covering everything from proprietary material to manufacturing processes, but two of them were going to expire in September of 2005, and we knew we'd have several category competitors waiting in the wings.

So we jumped in and earmarked several million dollars for commercial development. The first Flexon ad was expensive but was only fifteen seconds long and surprisingly simple in its message. The spot showed a close-up of a pair of hands holding and twisting a Flexon frame, as the voiceover asked, "When was the last time you saw something amazing? That *is* amazing!" It turned out to be extremely effective and fueled even more growth for the brand.

Initially, we started doing TV ads on local cable outlets in tandem with regional optical chains. The results were so impressive that Dave Chute proposed ramping it up with a campaign in connection with Lenscrafters in the summer of 1996. We ran about $3 million in cable TV advertising during a six-week period and our sales doubled, from 40,000 units per month to 80,000.

Everything seemed to fall into place at around that time. David Letterman, who had already graced the cover of *Rolling Stone* wearing Flexon, was later photographed wearing the frame on the cover of *Esquire* magazine, and Bill Gates was photographed for *Time* also wearing it.

There was, however, one very unfortunate gaffe that no one could have anticipated. We were producing Flexon print ads for consumer and trade publications to highlight the uniqueness of the Flexon material and, in the case of the trade, to preview our cable TV campaigns. The ads were done as illustrations; one featured a skyscraper bending backward as if to avoid a jet airliner flying near it with the headline, "If Only All Metal were Flexon". That particular ad was scheduled to run in the August/September 2001 timeframe. When the tragedy of September 11th occurred, a number of the publications running the ad had been published or were in production. We managed to pull a few of the placements, but that couldn't compensate for the terrible optics. There was a rumor going around that we were contacted by the FBI shortly after that episode, but neither I nor my partners ever received such a call.

Our original advertising agency, Arthur Kramer Advertising, was closed in the late 1980s when Arthur Kramer chose to retire. Sensing an opportunity and consistent with our approach to tackling just about any challenge we faced, we decided not to pursue outside ad/marketing resources and instead open an in-house agency with Donna and her team managing the operation. Their work included development of all advertising, collateral materials, in-store merchandising and packaging design. Later on, we added a public relations subsidiary under the direction of Robert Schienberg.

It had become very apparent to all of us that an important key to Marchon's continued success would depend upon our ability to continuously create "Wow!" factors for both our trade and consumer accounts. One thing we especially prided ourselves on was thinking about this marketing approach differently than other eyewear companies. We wanted to be viewed on the world stage like many other major consumer products brands.

The special ingredient to creating that dynamic is celebrity. An eyeglass or sunglass on the face of a famous person can virtually assure success. We went after celebs with panache and sex appeal to be our endorsers and ambassadors. Vendela, the Scandinavian model, became one of the faces of Marchon, as did the actress, Jane Seymour, to promote our Tres Jolie collection. Bo Derek was also a Marchon booster, and we even touted Sean "Puffy" Combs, the designer of our Sean John Eyewear line.

And much more followed. Through Robert Schienberg's tireless efforts, we were able to have Marchon products featured on "Ellen" a number of times, and also on "The View". But the homerun for us was being on "The Oprah Winfrey Show" in a big way. It turns out that Oprah was a Marchon fan herself (she was photographed wearing one of our Fendi styles), and we were able to appear on one of her "Oprah's Favorite Things for Summer" segments. Backstage, ten Marchon sales reps set up "Oprah's Sunglass Boutique," and then fit three-hundred-fifty audience members with our sunwear.

From that point on we pursued every high-visibility celebrity venue that we could. Marchon made it to the Academy Awards, the Grammys, the Kids' Choice Awards and the Screen Actors Guild Awards, eventually finding our way to the Cannes Film Festival and other international events. We wouldn't do swag or gift bags, but we'd deal with each celebrity individually. For example, we got actresses Helen Mirren and Cate Blanchett to wear Marchon during the Oscars.

We quickly became, in my estimation, the most successful eyewear company anywhere in getting A-list faces to wear our frames, to the point where it became a signature marketing device for us. Eventually we were spending about $40 million total on marketing and advertising each year, about evenly divided between consumer and trade campaigns. (My wife pointed out to me that, while I was being hailed as a marketing maverick within the optical industry, I would almost never walk into a retail store.)

Marchon's marketing lived up to its products, and its products lived up to their marketing. It was our commitment to great marketing in support of great products that, in essence, paved the way for us to pursue designer brands and lead to the company becoming a global player.

CHAPTER 7

THE MOST ALL-AMERICAN DESIGNER BRAND

MOST EYEWEAR COMPANIES were not very invested in high-profile designer names back in the early 1980s. Certainly that was the case at Avant Garde during our tenure, and for several years after. Eyewear and the optical industry were just beginning to transition from a medical field to a fashion milieu in the U.S. Europe, of course, was a whole other story.

Our new company was very deliberately built on a foundation of "house" brands, which is how we viewed Marcolin and Marchon. With some exceptions (most notably Christian Dior, Diane Von Furstenberg, Polo Ralph Lauren, Gloria Vanderbilt and a few others that had licensed their names to eyewear companies), the market was primarily dominated by house brands.

Licensed brands cost royalty monies, and who really wanted to pay them? Was there any brand that could be affixed to eyewear that would make a difference in sales? And for that matter, could a solid designer name simply be "affixed" to a temple, or was there much more involved?

That all changed for us in 1988. Luxottica, which had built its U.S. distribution arm, Avant Garde, into a true market leader, announced in dramatic fashion that the company had signed an agreement with internationally famous designer, Giorgio Armani, to introduce an eyewear collection worldwide bearing his name and brand. Additionally, the collection would be designed by Armani himself and would reflect vintage styling.

Up until that time, most eyewear collections featured larger eye sizes. Armani changed that, too. His premier collection was comprised of much smaller styles, many in round shapes. To be honest, nobody really fell in love with that first collection, but that was beside the point. Luxottica had a designer brand with worldwide visibility and a designer who was actively involved in the eyewear's creation.

They also had a clever marketing strategy: rather than make Armani available to every optical location in the U.S. market, they restricted distribution to only their "best" accounts—which made the vast majority want it even more.

The Armani Eyewear brand was an instant hit even if the first collection didn't overwhelm. It didn't take its success to make us realize that we would have to get into the designer category in a big way.

We had a few licensing relationships: one with Disney, for example, to create a children's eyewear line, and two brands we obtained through the acquisition of a small eyewear distributor called Vertice—Fendi and Alexander Julian—both for the U.S. market only. But the lion's share of our revenue at that time was generated by the Marchon and Marcolin house brands.

It became apparent that we needed a brand that had global value and recognition, and would pave the way for Marchon internationally. Outside of the U.S., Marchon was not a readily recognized name as we had virtually no presence in overseas markets. But a big designer brand could open those doors for us.

At that time in the early 1990s, the big casual apparel manufacturer and retailer, Guess International, was in the hunt for a good eyewear licensee and their research led them to Marchon and our powerful competitor, Viva. Coincidentally, we also learned that Calvin Klein was considering a new eyewear partner.

The Calvin Klein brand had been on the rise for some time, having impacted categories like ready-to-wear, jeans and fragrances. And Calvin himself was a marketing visionary, although his marketing occasionally stirred up some controversy.

In 1980, a flirtatious fifteen-year-old Brooke Shields was featured in print ads shot by Richard Avedon and a TV commercial adorned in skintight Calvin Klein Jeans; she had one line of dialogue: "You know what comes between me and my Calvins? Nothing." The censors at CBS found the commercial too provocative and refused to take it. ABC then followed suit. Regardless, Calvin's jeans skyrocketed as did Brooke Shields' career.

When Calvin decided to introduce sexy men's underwear, he hired Mark Wahlberg (then known as Marky Mark) to wear them sticking out of his jeans on billboards and in ads appearing all over the country. And he followed that up by putting his underwear on a number of celebrity models and Hollywood actors.

As it happened, Calvin Klein had an eyewear licensee that was a major competitor of ours. But the relationship soured when it became clear to Calvin (who is very much a hands-on designer with every project he undertakes, and had many distinct ideas about how eyewear should be done) that this particular eyewear distributor had his way of "doing things," and was not receptive to suggestions from someone outside the optical industry. So when the short-term contract on the brand expired, it was not renewed. That was followed by a brief agreement with another European distributor that ended after a year when the two parties couldn't agree on just about anything.

Despite these setbacks, Calvin remained very intrigued by eyewear. He would frequent the Columbus Avenue, Manhattan-based shop of a prominent optician named Robert Marc. Robert was well-known for having a fashion sensibility that was innovative, creative and out of the mainstream. In fact, Robert's was one of the first eyewear boutiques in New York City and attracted a number of celebrities.

When they first met and discussed what Calvin was looking for in his eyewear personally, Robert had just the thing. He had acquired a cache of frames that had been sold in Great Britain's socialized vision care program and Calvin absolutely loved them. According to Robert, he wound up buying the whole inventory.

From that point on, a solid friendship was formed between Calvin and Robert that lasted for many years. Calvin would stop in at Robert's shop simply to talk eyewear. He shared with him the details of his rocky relationships with his previous distributors, and it was immediately clear to Robert that Calvin didn't want to be restricted by conventional practices in creating and marketing eyewear.

This was a key tenet of Calvin's fashion design philosophy, as he had proved with fragrances and jeans. Do it in your own, unique way and bring something new to the party. Of course, I could see how that would be difficult for some in our business to swallow.

We had made some inroads with the Calvin Klein organization and made it known that Marchon would be interested in vying for the opportunity to create and market Calvin Klein Eyewear. The company had a senior vice president in charge of retail development and licensing named Marty Staff and he had become somewhat involved. But we recognized that it really came down to satisfying Calvin himself.

In order to get a seat at the table, we mixed and matched a variety of different frame elements from existing collections—the temples of one with the frame front of another—to simulate what the Calvin Klein Eyewear brand might look like.

Ironically, the Viva Group was also in the running for the Calvin license and also presented some prototypes. In fact, we were both competing for two big brands—Calvin and Guess. Viva was working with a much-respected Italian eyewear designer named Sergio Cereda, which gave them something of a competitive distinction. Nonetheless, it appeared that we had the Guess license lined up, but we wanted to hold out for Calvin. And as fate would have it, each licensee probably got the brand that was best suited to them; Viva got Guess and built it into an incredible business. We got Calvin, although it took some hard work on our part.

Calvin had shown Robert our prototypes, as well as Viva's, and asked him to make a recommendation on who would be his best partner. Apparently, Robert had a better sense of Viva's capabilities through his knowledge of Cereda's work and reputation, but was later impressed to learn that Marchon had the expertise and reputation of Marcolin's manufacturing prowess as well as that of top Japanese factories behind it.

Robert, however, was no pushover. After reviewing our samples and Viva's, he arranged meetings for both companies at the Calvin Klein offices. Jeff White and I carried the Marchon flag.

The meeting started out a little contentiously. "Your samples are all created from the various parts of other companies' frames," he said bluntly. "All you did was take off the logos."

With a little frustration in our voices, we said, "The samples were only a way of conveying what we thought a Calvin Klein collection might look like."

Eventually, after a number of meetings and the creation of another set of manufactured prototypes—based on more obscure styles that Robert gave us for reference—he voted in favor of Marchon.

Thus began our relationship with Calvin Klein and, as well, Robert Marc, who would become a very valuable asset to Marchon. Robert is very animated and very knowledgeable, and his excitement for eyewear can be infectious.

When we finally signed the licensing agreement, Calvin said to us, "I've given you the golden key." He knew what he had, and he bestowed it upon Marchon.

Calvin was very intimately involved in the creation of the collection from the very beginning, to the point where he could become something of a micro-manager (quite an irony coming from me). But to his credit, he knew when he needed help, so he hired Robert to manage the relationship with Marchon and contribute to designing the collection. He explained his vision to Robert and the two of them, with the help of Marcolin manufacturing, created the collection together. Calvin was 100% in charge of what we were doing.

Calvin brought a new aesthetic to eyewear and he changed our business dramatically. That aesthetic had a clear image which was derived from the Calvin Klein brand. Clean, minimalistic, yet sophisticated, elegant and modern. These are great adjectives that could be used to describe virtually any Calvin Klein product, and they described our eyewear collection.

There were a number of ways in which Calvin Klein and Marchon were compatible: similar mindsets, similar objectives, and similar market positions. Calvin was classically American; and the Marchon sensibility was also classically American.

It also enhanced our market positioning versus our biggest competitor, Luxottica. Armani was an Italian designer and brand, licensed by an Italian eyewear company. Calvin was an American designer and brand, licensed now by a thoroughly American company. The parallels were not lost on most people, and just served to reinforce the Marchon folklore.

We definitely wanted to go head-to-head with Armani for a number of reasons. Both brands aspired to higher goals. Calvin Klein Eyewear would cost us more to make—first in the Marcolin factories of Italy and later on, when we introduced titanium eyewear, the great factories of Japan. True designer quality at a higher price point.

It would also cost us more to market and sell. Calvin had very distinct ideas about how the line should be presented, sold and merchandised, which was largely consistent with the other products in his portfolio.

He was also very meticulous about how products were made. He insisted that we always work with his colors and shapes for each season. We came up with an integrated spring hinge; Calvin didn't like the solder points. We did a very expensive stainless steel collection that didn't excite him, so we went back to the drawing board. We wanted to be a great licensee, and we knew it was our job to maximize our licensor relationship.

We had hired Linda Laube (via the Vertice acquisition) and made her brand manager for Calvin Klein Eyewear. It was her challenge to meet with Calvin and his team several times a year to do a complete line review. He was a great person, but you never forgot who was calling the shots.

Although he could be a stern taskmaster, I felt fortunate to work closely with Calvin himself. We were ready to work with a designer that could bring a whole new perspective to the company, and he was the right person at the right time. Going forward, Marchon would never be the same.

To his great credit, Calvin was not averse to bringing on the best people he could if it involved a product category outside of his design expertise. In the case of eyewear, he turned once again to Robert Marc, and asked him to take charge of his eyewear collection. And that was the start of a remarkable collaboration that would last for fifteen years. Calvin had a vision and he would share it with Robert, who would do the designing.

Robert became a valued advisor to Marchon as well. He served as liaison between Calvin, me and the Marchon team. He would attend our sales meetings and present the newest collection to the reps. He would work with Giancarla Agnoli at the Marcolin factory to assist production. He would even go to Calvin Klein fashion shoots on "eyewear day," and fit Kate Moss or Christy Turlington with the latest styles for our advertising photos.

We assembled our Calvin Klein sales team by tapping some of our current top reps and hiring others who had the skill set and the discipline necessary.

There were many requirements to becoming a Calvin Klein rep. It was mandatory that you wear Calvin Klein apparel. There were guidelines for how the product was to be presented, sold and merchandised, and it forced all of us to be extremely precise. There was a particular protocol for everything—product, marketing, execution, education. The Calvin Klein organization actually had a manual that spelled out the protocols.

There were even guidelines for the accounts. Your store had to merchandise Calvin the way he envisioned, and the display materials and posters had to be used properly. If a rep walked into an account and saw only three Calvin Klein styles on the frame board, she was to close that account down.

This all made for a volatile time for our sales force. While many were thrilled and honored to be selected to sell Calvin, there were those who so distained the rigid procedures that they wouldn't go near it.

Also, as we had done with Marcolin, representing Calvin Klein in the field meant creating another sales team. As I mentioned, this caused resentment among some reps because it meant yet another in-house "competitor" going after their business with a hot designer brand. And if the resentment was valid, it was on us to figure out how to address it.

We realized that you couldn't simply remove an asset like Calvin from a rep's territory without accounting for it. So we came up with a compensation plan that, although a greater expense to the company for a short period, would cover any deficit that losing Calvin created and also provide an additional 1.5% override on the Calvin sales in the territory. At the end of the year, the rep would be making more money than he did previously, which went a long way to showing that the additional rep was a positive solution.

We signed the license for Calvin Klein in 1991 and then had about eighteen months to build the collection. In the fall of '92, we soft launched the collection at Vision Expo West in Las Vegas (all our male reps had to wear gray flannel Calvin suits) and intended to start shipping in early '93. In between, we staged a launch party that was unprecedented in the optical business.

Calvin was the marketing master, and I was fortunate to work closely with him and learn from him. It became clear, as he kept pushing us and pushing us, that he liked to do things on a grand scale, and he had quite a grand idea for our launch party. We rented out the Tony Shafrazi Art Gallery in the Chelsea section of New York City on 26th Street. Shafrazi was very cutting-edge and a little controversial, representing artists like Keith Haring and Jean-Michel Basquiat.

Then he hired New York's preeminent party planner, Robert Isabell, to work his magic. Isabell was well-known for creating spectacular events for Steve Rubell and Ian Schrager at the peak of Studio 54's notoriety, White House Christmas events during the Clinton Administration and numerous Kennedy family weddings.

The first thing Isabell did for our party was to have all the art removed from the walls and replaced with custom-made eyewear displays. Then he decorated the displays with virtually every Calvin Klein eyewear and sunwear style we had. Between that and models wearing nearly nothing more than body paint, it was quite a scene.

Then Calvin prepared the guest list. Not unlike Studio 54, the invitation list included every celebrity, media maven and New York luminary he knew—more than four-hundred of them. We had made a commitment early on in the relationship with Calvin to dedicate all our resources to the collection's success, but I have to admit that when I learned how much the party would cost us, I almost passed out.

Additionally, Calvin decided that we should give every guest a pair of Calvin Klein eyewear or sunwear. To do so, we had Robert Marc and his optical staff fit all four-hundred party guests. They didn't get a break for hours.

After that, Calvin Klein Eyewear took off like a house on fire. We came up with a two-tiered plan in which the top-tier optical retailers got to carry styles that were exclusive to them. Eventually we also line-extended into the CK Collection, a more daring, exciting and younger collection that we made in China, and Calvin Klein Black Label, a higher-end offshoot brand. Within a decade's time, the Calvin Klein division of Marchon exceeded $140 million in sales.

Calvin Klein, the man and the brand, stepped up Marchon's game dramatically. The relationship was based on far more than a designer name on a frame temple. The Calvin Klein approach and business philosophy was soon overlaid on the Marchon framework. We adopted the Calvin view of the world—regarding fashion, image and marketing—and his view of the eyeglass and sunglass markets. Most importantly, we embraced his expectations about how the product was to be presented to retail, and how it was to be presented *at* retail.

It was also very gratifying for me to have earned Calvin's appreciation and respect. I had asked Donna Rollins to hire a film crew to make a short film in which she interviewed Calvin for the sales team and for our introduction of the collection at Vision Expo West. "Al Berg did a fantastic job with this launch," he told her when the filming was over.

In the immediate years that followed the introduction of Calvin Klein, many new imperatives emerged for Marchon.

Certainly it was evident that designer branding and influences would be an integral part of the eyewear agenda permanently. And with Calvin as our calling card, we were able to secure a number of top fashion brands of the time—Donna Karan, Michael Kors and Coach to name a few. Each one was attracted to us as a licensee because of what we had accomplished with Calvin Klein, and of course they wanted the same treatment. Interestingly, every time we added a new designer brand it changed the culture of the company and involved something of a learning curve.

To assist us, we turned to Robert Marc to help manage our new designer relationships and with the creation of their eyewear collections. Every designer, that is, except Calvin, as Robert was already in his service.

Our feeling about brands was that "fewer and better" was the right formula for us. Every time we saw a competitor introduce yet another "B" level brand we'd be thrilled.

Calvin Klein Eyewear also opened up a whole new customer category for us—department stores. Calvin was committed to taking advantage of his brand equity by having us start a retail sunglasses business that would share the department store shelves with his fragrances and apparel.

We had some presence in the sunwear field largely due to prescription sunglasses sold at optical, but this was a whole new world. We opened a showroom in New York's Bryant Park neighborhood and went about courting this new account base. And as Calvin's eyewear so motivated other designers to enter the arena with us, so too did his sunwear. It quickly became a given with the launch of Donna Karan or Michael Kors Eyewear, that retail sunglasses would be an essential part of the plan.

Success begets success, and soon we were attracting other world-class licenses. We started researching new product categories for

Marchon, and sports-related eyewear and sunwear seemed like a logical opportunity. And the biggest world-class brand in that space was Nike, a real category-killer. I was thoroughly convinced that you couldn't enter a category with enormous potential by taking a third- rate brand and trying to make it into a first-rate brand, as so many of our competitors attempted to do.

The challenge with Nike, as it was to some extent with Calvin early on, was that their management had a vision about how they wanted to build their eyewear brand that we knew wouldn't work with the retail optical marketplace. They were using the business model that they had employed with athletic footwear, creating a price structure that would produce almost no margin at all for the distributor and retailer.

Part of our mission was to show Nike that we should marry our skills in eyewear with their skills as marketers, but that the sneaker model would fail. They didn't take into account how very different the two businesses are. They'd ship their footwear products on pallets, and take huge quantity orders six months in advance, completely antithetical to how optical works. Eventually, we convinced them that if the two companies applied their specific strengths, everyone would get what they wanted.

Prior to Marchon, Nike was producing plano, or non-prescription, sunglasses on their own. We wanted to take over that business and also add an eyeglasses component. And that's were Flexon came in. We had a great product in Flexon that we felt would work very well with the Nike brand, and the Nike people agreed. Working with their design and technology team we created a new design for Flexon that was Nike-only, so to speak. It was one of the few times that Nike was willing to co-brand. We were able to build a product and a category that was appropriate to the brand, and Nike became a success in the eyewear/sunwear space.

But with brands like Calvin Klein and Nike, the U.S. and North American markets were too small a stage for us. It was Calvin's plan, and ours, that in order to succeed we'd have to think globally. And the Calvin Klein brand, in particular, was our gateway to other markets around the world. While the Marchon brand was not so broadly known, Calvin was gaining momentum all over the world. In fact, survey results showed that his brand was as well-known as Pepsi.

So that was one of our new imperatives: go global and lead the charge with Calvin Klein. By the end of the 20th century, we were well on our way to achieving those goals.

Marchon co-presidents Al Berg, Jeff White and Larry Roth with a super-sized Fuzzy mascot at the grand opening of our Melville, N.Y. headquarters. Jeff was incredible at creating our physical and operational facilities.
(All photos courtesy of Donna Rollins and Marchon unless otherwise noted.)

Giovanni Marcolin Coffen, the patriarch of Marcolin Eyewear was an ideal partner for Marchon. His company provided us with incredible products, particularly in our formative days. (Courtesy of Marcolin Eyewear)

The original Marchon logo featuring the iconic red "O", often represented in the company's marketing by the Marchon Fuzzies and red roses displayed at the company's trade show booths.

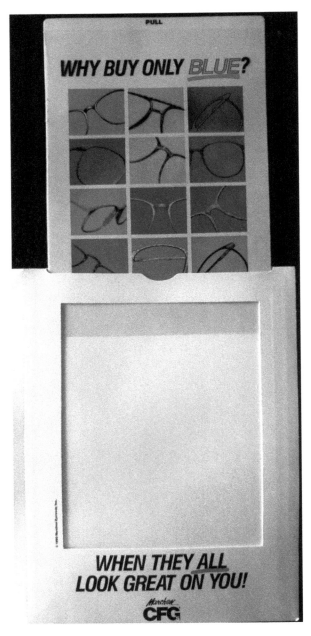

CFG (carbon fiber graphite) was an incredible hit for the young Marchon Eyewear. The material was lightweight and the color possibilities were almost endless, as illustrated by our "Magic Window" collateral piece.

SOME EARLIER ATTEMPTS AT FLEXIBLE FRAMES

TV campaign begins
august 23

If only all metal were
FLEXON
by MARCHON

Flexon Eyewear was a revolutionary product and we had a lot of fun with the marketing, as this Flexon brochure cover (right) depicts. We took heat for our "bending building" announcement ad which debuted just a few weeks before 9/11.

Al with '90s supermodel, Vendala (left) and with Larry and Bo Derek during Vision Expo. Celebrity endorsements helped to create a "Wow!" factor for Marchon that our customers loved.

Al with Diane Von Furstenberg and Calvin Klein. The licensing agreement with Calvin in 1992 put Marchon on a whole new playing field and paved the way for global expansion.

Marchon featured on "Ellen" with the introduction of our Emilio Pucci Eyewear collection. Daytime TV was a great marketing vehicle.

Giancarla Agnoli receiving a hug from designer Donna Karan. Giancarla helped drive Marchon's global campaign and became the head of our entire Italian operation and eventually all of Europe.

Celebrating Marchon's Twenty-Fifth Anniversary with Larry addressing the sales team at our annual meeting in Cancun. The Anniversary logo adorned just about every print or marketing item that year.

Luxottica's Leonardo Del Vecchio was the most powerful competitor Marchon ever faced and in many ways served as a mentor to me. (Courtesy of Luxottica Group.)

Al with VSP Vision Care's CEO, Rob Lynch, shortly after VSP's 2008 acquisition of Marchon was announced, creating a $3.3 billion business with international expansion plans. (Courtesy of VSP Global.)

CHAPTER **8**

GOING GLOBAL

SHORTLY AFTER THE launch of Calvin Klein Eyewear, we turned our attention to the world beyond our U.S. borders. Calvin was attempting to become a global brand, and we recognized that both he and we were looking to a more extensive playing field. It became an imperative.

The major European players—Luxottica, Safilo, Marcolin and several others—were all looking at the eyewear marketplace on a global scale. They had all opened beachheads in a number of other countries. Marcolin, for example, had solid distribution relationships in about five countries like Germany, Switzerland and England, and they were very excited to bring Calvin Klein to those markets. In order for Marchon to be viewed as equal to these aggressive international players, we had to follow suit.

Also, we knew that if we wanted to continue to sign marquee brands to our portfolio, we would need to be perceived as a global competitor with the resources to succeed overseas. Signing Calvin played a big part in creating that perception. Our strong domestic business provided the resources. The global footprint we'd create would do the rest.

It was clear to us that the overwhelming majority of American competitors were very parochial—they couldn't see much outside the U.S. Those that were "selling" in Europe or Asia were doing so in a catch-as-catch-can manner, meaning they'd attend the international trade shows and hope to sell a handful of frames to local optical retailers. Other U.S. competitors avoided the global play altogether, and to a degree it kept them out of the global brands war. What they didn't realize was that eventually that war would come to them.

We needed to have a plan to, as they say, go big or go home. We knew that just selling off inventory from a trade show booth was not the answer. We needed to establish a full-scale sales, marketing and distribution business in each of the markets we hoped to open and service. And we needed to do research in order to execute the plan. In some cases, we came to recognize, we'd need design facilities and even Marchon-controlled manufacturing resources, depending upon the market and what we hoped to accomplish.

Consistent with Marcolin's approach, our plan of attack was to take Calvin global, in effect leading with the brand that already had some franchise overseas; Europeans knew Calvin as a celebrity though not necessarily as a fashion designer. There was definitely name recognition, albeit not as ubiquitous as Giorgio Armani's.

To begin the journey, I turned to a number of our people to create an international team, but three in particular—Fred Humphrey, who had run our education programs but was also vital in the U.S. rollout of Calvin; Deb Ingino, our customer service maven, and Giancarla Agnoli, the Marcolin export manager who was becoming more and more integral to the Marchon mission each day. As Larry had our domestic business well in hand, I committed myself to leading the international charge.

We looked at the world, analyzed the countries that made sense and where we could learn enough to properly partner up. The English-speaking countries were a logical choice, and we wound up launching Marchon Canada and Marchon U.K. ourselves, along with Central and South America which we managed (as we did Canada) out of our offices in New York. Marcolin was a great ally in managing international markets, and wound up handling the five countries for us where they had strength. In each market, we researched the key distribution players and sought out those who would make the strongest, most compatible partners for us.

Within eighteen months, we had established distribution in ten countries, and we soon were looking beyond Europe to Asia and Australia. South Korea, for example, became a very strong market for us.

Admittedly, some markets presented obstacles. Russia and Eastern Europe we knew would be tricky, so we made it a lower priority. In the Middle East, which presented many complexities, we were fortunate to find a solid distributor who entered into a joint venture with us.

In some markets, we were able to solve the distribution challenge by forming unique partnerships. In Indonesia, for example, there was an eye doctor who owned a multi-location, high-fashion retail business which he named for himself, Aboe Optical. That became our entry to that market.

Ultimately, we pursued the countries which we believed could afford the product, projected a strong sense of fashion and were receptive to designer brands.

Fred was a critical figure in our international expansion, although remarkably he had no international business background. But like me, he was very entrepreneurial and could uncover the resources to get things done. Together, we came up with a strategy to open countries one-by-one. Fred would travel to those countries on fact-finding missions to learn the structure of their markets, who the key movers and shakers were in wholesale distribution and retail, and the cultural or style preference distinctions. He would also tell the Marchon and Calvin Klein stories to everyone he'd meet.

Additionally, Fred happened upon a unique optical business model that was prevalent in Scandinavia. Apparently many wholesale distributors were also retailers, in effect vertically integrating for greater efficiencies. Selecting these types of businesses to represent us to their wholesale customers brought with it immediate access to their own stores.

As a case in point, there's a large, optical wholesale/retail operation in Sweden called Synsam. They were a distributor and a successful, high-brand-recognition chain retailer. Today, they have over five-hundred doors throughout Scandinavia, with a large concentration in Sweden.

With a little research, Fred soon learned that Synsam had a great reputation and a remarkable 35% market share. We both knew that they'd make a great partner and the relationship turned out to be a gold mine. We went to the other Nordic countries to find other business models similar to Synsam's and made them distributors as well.

As we became smarter about the international markets, we realized that there were three ways for us to establish a beachhead in any particular country—joint venture distributorship, full partner distributorship or corporately owned distributorship. The key was flexibility.

In the United Kingdom, to cite one example, Marcolin had coverage but it turned out it wasn't very robust. So we chose to revise our original plan, and enter the U.K. with a corporately owned operation. Fred spent a fair amount of time in Britain and found a great headquarters location in a town called Peasmarch, about fifty miles northwest of London. The town also featured a quaint, 16th century inn (converted to a bed and breakfast) and he negotiated an exceptional rate on rooms for the U.S. team members who visited frequently.

That part of Britain was experiencing an economic downturn at the time, so Fred went to the local unemployment agency to find people for the warehouse, customer service and clerical. Deb Ingino had gone to Peasmarch to assist Fred in the launch and met a young lady who worked as a clerk at the inn. Deb noticed that she had great rapport with the guests and other staff members, along with a real entrepreneurial spirit. She immediately offered her a job. Eventually, she became our director of operations for all of Europe. The resume mattered less to us than the person's quality.

For us, experience was less important than potential and the entrepreneurial instinct. We hired many of our overseas people based on that criterion.

Overall, our vision for the international rollout was to replicate in those other markets what Marchon had accomplished in the U.S.; in effect, to create a series of what I sometimes referred to as "mini-Marchons" throughout the world.

Our plan called for much more than simply exporting our products and marketing. We wanted to export the Marchon philosophy—the high service levels of our sales and customer service reps, the urgency to ship orders out same-day, and to help the retail customer sell-through.

While the Marchon way caught on in a number of the countries we entered, there were a few that pushed back on this "American style" of doing business. The Netherlands was a good case in point.

When we'd interview job candidates in the Netherlands, we were consistently surprised about their expressed priorities. Very few candidates asked about salary. They were far more interested in knowing about our pension plan and the number of days off for vacation and holidays.

One of our good contacts in the Netherlands finally explained it to us: "We work to live," he said. "You guys live to work." (By the way, the employment laws in the Netherlands and a number of other countries were alien to us because they were often so unfavorable to the employer. I sent Robert Feldman to fire an employee in the Netherlands and that termination ultimately cost us $300,000 to settle.)

The Calvin Klein launch presented some other cultural hurdles. As with the U.S. rollout, we had a mandate to train the sales reps in each country in the proper way to sell Calvin. Likewise, the customer had to be trained about how to present it.

For the majority of salespeople in our international outposts, this was unprecedented. The idea of being trained to sell eyewear, much less to follow a designer's strict set of rules to do so, was a brand new experience. But for the most part, the sales teams appreciated it. And Fred trained them all, from the locations managed by Marcolin to the joint ventures and company-owned distributors.

It was our view that the attributes that made Marchon U.S. successful—the training and marketing, the strict dedication to customer service, and our American perspective—could work in other countries. And the answer is, they did.

We appealed to the salespeople to trust us, to trust in our way of doing things and they got on board. They came to acknowledge that

Marchon had a unique reputation for success, and they wanted to be a part of it. It helped us stand out and it certainly helped us attract better salespeople. And what became a worldwide success with Calvin Klein Eyewear helped us to attract other premium fashion brands.

Without a doubt, Calvin opened the doors for us to international markets and allowed us to follow with other products, such as Flexon. Of course, we still had much to learn about product preferences among these myriad cultures. It came down to taste and fit.

In some cases, taste or style preferences were a little idiosyncratic (France, for example, seemed wedded to the Cat Eye), but could be otherwise addressed with design and coloration adjustments. Fit, however, was a different story, particularly in the Asian markets.

Europe and America are very similar. But Asia, particularly Japan and South Korea, where we cultivated a strong distribution, was more complicated. The people of the East, typically, were not very forthcoming with their opinions, while the people of the West, especially we Americans, were very direct with ours. Hence, it was hard to get a good read on the Asian markets.

In time, we realized that the countries of Asia had a unique set of conditions that had to be met in order to succeed. Their fashion and color preferences were often very different than those in Europe and America. We set up a design and distribution center in Japan to service our Asian partners and to create "Asian fit" eyewear styles. We also opened a distribution center in Hong Kong. Later on, we entered into a joint venture with our Japanese manufacturing partner, Nakanishi, to open a manufacturing facility in mainland China, primarily for the production of Flexon.

As the international business expanded, it became obvious that we couldn't operate all those outposts from New York. We originally had small warehouses to supply each of our markets, but later on recognized that opening up centralized facilities would be more efficient and more cost-effective. So we opened large distribution centers in Amsterdam and Italy. Italy's facilities also featured a design center and both were managed by Giancarla Agnoli, who, by then, had left Marcolin to join

Marchon as a full-time employee after the two companies separated. (Giancarla would finally go on to run our entire European operation.)

With the switch to centralized overseas distribution, we wound up having to lay off seventy-five to one-hundred employees who had been working in the small, local warehouses, which became a really daunting task due to the varied labor laws within each country.

It also became apparent very quickly that we'd have to create a certain amount of autonomy for these markets, because we couldn't be looking over their shoulders from thousands of miles away. So billing, for example, was transferred from the U.S. to each of our countries. Computer systems as well—they had to jibe with our American operation but obviously accommodate the special needs of each overseas business.

One aspect of our operation we were committed to presenting uniformly throughout the world was Marchon marketing. If the Calvin Klein rollout taught us anything, it was that maintaining a consistent image, messaging and presentation throughout all we did was paramount. It worked for us in the United States, and we were pretty sure it would work in our international markets as well.

We were largely correct in that view. The people we hired were very receptive to our approach, as they hadn't experienced anything like it prior. Nobody was "doing Marchon" overseas, and that alone gave us a distinct advantage.

Our level of success varied from market to market. In England, for example, we were an immediate hit and became the third biggest supplier there within three years. Other markets took off more slowly.

As we went about opening new countries, we remained very precise in our planning, making sure our research was on target. Sometimes we'd hold up launches if conditions weren't perfectly right, as when we'd agree to partner with a distributor only to find that he misrepresented his company's stature or performance. (We met a number of prospective distributors who would tell us, "I'm the number one guy in the market".)

You had to remember that continued expansion would contain

many variables. For example, we were preparing to open Germany as a joint venture when the agreement with our distribution partner was terminated. We were still committed to opening in six weeks, so we sent over Deb Ingino and others from the international team to set things up. They needed to hire a staff and help obtain a facility. Using cell phones and working out of their hotel, they interviewed just about everyone they could—bartenders, babysitters, *hausfraus*. It was all hands on deck and we made the deadline.

Marchon's global offensive required a substantial investment of our resources, and we couldn't have done it without a strong and highly profitable domestic business. Profitability overseas would be difficult and take time to achieve. Costs, as one might anticipate, were much higher in the international markets but the product was also priced higher.

However, profitability was not our primary or immediate objective. The priority was to build out a global footprint and create a global company, goals I'm proud to say we achieved. Within a short time after going global, Marchon became a world-class player, sharing the stage with Luxottica and Safilo. And ours was the only company of this scope to be based in the U.S.

It was our objective to generate company-wide sales based on 50% optical goods and 50% sunwear, split 50% domestic, 50% international. We got it to roughly 40% international sales and profits, 60% U.S.

But we had obtained a new plateau in Marchon's success, thanks in large part to Calvin Klein. The launch of Calvin Klein Eyewear made global expansion necessary. It also captured the attention of a number of other designers and design houses and positioned Marchon as a desirable prospective licensee. Within a few years we developed, in addition to partnerships with Donna Karan, Michael Kors and Coach, licensing agreements with Oscar de la Renta, Sean John, Pucci and Karl Lagerfeld to name a few. Calvin gave rise to our reputation for being true to the design and marketing credo of the licensor. As Donna Karan said to us, "I want the Calvin Klein treatment".

As I had mentioned, Calvin also nudged us into a whole new

revenue stream with retail sunglasses. While we had some sunwear in our collections up to that point, it was never as prominent as it became under the Calvin Klein label. Calvin viewed sunwear as an accessory comparable to handbags and bracelets, and gave us access to better department stores and specialty retailers. To support this new business, we opened a New York City showroom and created a separate retail sales division.

With this larger profile came an interest on the part of large retailers, both optical and non-optical, to pursue private label programs with us, which gave birth to a private label subsidiary, Allure Eyewear.

As we prepared to enter the 21st century, we looked back on what we had accomplished with unabashed pride. In less than two decades, we managed to create a large and very substantial eyewear company. And we changed the industry paradigm both domestically and overseas.

But Marchon had reached a point in its lifecycle where the three owners could no longer preside over every aspect of the business by themselves. It became necessary to create a new level of management and imbue it with the decision making authority to take some control.

As entrepreneurs who had been intimately involved with every aspect of our business, this was new and unfamiliar territory. But we felt confident that there was a bright future ahead.

CHAPTER 9

THE PERFECT STORM

THE COMPANY HAD come a long way by the time we celebrated Marchon's Twentieth Anniversary in 2003. In those two decades our revenue had grown more than one hundred-fold, to a little over $350 million. Our staff grew significantly also, from twenty-four employees to well over a thousand. Marchon had evolved from a company of house brands into a major supplier of licensed brands that carried worldwide recognition, matched by our worldwide distribution footprint. Ours had become the first and only American company to join the ranks of Luxottica and Safilo as global competitors.

With our rapid global expansion, the explosion of designer brands, and our creating products expressly for different countries, we were experiencing sales growth at the rate, in my estimation, of $20 million to $30 million per year. We believed that we could reach $1 billion in sales some time into the new decade.

What was even more remarkable was that in those twenty years, we never had a fiscal challenge and never needed further capital beyond that initial $2 million investment. We were growing like the proverbial weed.

And the optical industry was very much keeping pace, particularly among the larger companies. Luxottica was diversifying dramatically in retail, wholesale and new technologies. Marcolin, now out on its own, was poised for continued growth. Safilo was very aggressive in the eyewear brand race.

On top of that there was the emergence of the Internet. This new communications and informational tool opened up many new opportunities for optical in the 21st century. As a result, some fourteen business-to-business web portals emerged, each to provide purchasing efficiencies to optical retail customers. Representatives from each portal came to see us. And each had pretty much the same message: put your product catalog on our site or risk going out of business.

I asked Jim McGrann, who was heading up our IT team as our CTO, to handle the vetting process and select a single web partner. He dug into it. I remember telling him, "Don't create Frankenstein's monster," meaning don't get Marchon into a relationship that could come back to bite us.

After going through this trial, we decided on partnering with VisionWeb, a portal with solid industry roots. Essilor, Johnson & Johnson and Luxottica had taken equity stakes in the venture, and Marchon soon joined them. Shortly after, it became apparent that our OfficeMate management system could be complementary to VisionWeb, a win-win for everyone.

Concurrently, we set up a purchasing portal of our own, largely to promote participation in a customer recognition program called Marchon Valued Partner (MVP). It allowed our accounts to order products on-line and also accrue co-op and marketing dollars, continuing education and prizes like Michael Kors handbags or Calvin Klein luggage, depending upon their volume and purchasing growth. We also ran contests through the website, like "Thanks a Bunch, You Win Lunch," in which the entire office staff received a lunch courtesy of their Marchon rep.

Not surprisingly, many accounts wanted the security and comfort of placing orders with the customer service reps they had come to know over many years, making MVP less than an immediate home run. But within two or three years, as the Internet became more pervasive, MVP became most accounts' preferred way of ordering and an ultimate success.

It was at this time that we came to an important realization: the days when three entrepreneurs alone, no matter how committed, could manage a company which had grown to this scope and complexity were over.

This was particularly apparent when you looked at our new international business. When you exclusively managed the domestic business, you were dealing with one country, one culture and one market. But the foreign markets were all different—different languages, different laws and business practices, different cultures, different infrastructures.

Our U.S. computer system, for example, was not designed or built to be used as one universal system in multiple overseas markets, so we had to modify it to accommodate those other markets. We went from operating one system to operating ten.

We entered 2003 trying to control explosive growth, deal with myriad new and unique problems and supervise a diverse group of managers, each following, to some extent, his or her separate agendas.

There was also frustration with our existing systems, which were great for America but weren't easily expanded overseas. To my mind our original systems were like the lower Manhattan of the 18th century—roads crisscrossing each other, taking winding paths—as opposed to upper Manhattan of the 19th century which had developed into a very well-organized grid.

After attending two different management retreats on Supply Chain and International Sales/Operations Management, my own frustrations hit a critical point. I wrote a memo to our team, recommending that they read it slowly in a quiet environment and digest its content.

I pointed out that they were probably frustrated and aggravated with their jobs, partially by the lack of adequate support systems, partially by the structure we had and partially by what I called the "territoriality" of some within the management team.

"It became obvious that if we are truly going to be a global player even close to Luxottica and Safilo, we urgently need to RE-ENGINEER the company from top to bottom," I wrote.

I went on to emphasize that we needed to have a Plan/Vision and that the steps in pursuit of that included completely revamping the supply chain from design through planning and ordering through production, developing a global vision for the company, integrating globally all our marketing functions and refining our budgeting and planning.

"We need better knowledge and communication within our entire team so that we all know what the vision is," I continued, pointing out that individual goals (territoriality) interfere with the company's overall goal. "The only acceptable answer going forward is the right answer for Marchon and not the right answer for any individual country, department or person."

I concluded the memo by saying that "in typical Al style" I would be letting some of them know when their approach to management seemed to be letting territoriality interfere with their success and the success of the company.

At around the same time, we had decided to recruit new, senior-level management because we were running this big operation and not doing it efficiently. We found individuals whom we felt were substantial, seasoned management people, and we gave them the authority, responsibility and decision making capability to allow them to do their jobs unfettered by politics or hierarchy. This was especially true on the international front. So for the first time Marchon had a chief operating officer (whom I was particularly impressed with when I put him in place) and a chief financial officer.

Early in that year, I was diagnosed with a heart condition that required surgery, and after that a fairly protracted convalescence. Of course, I was constantly in touch with the office, but in retrospect I realized that it wasn't quite the same as being the on-site operator.

Everything was becoming exponentially more complicated. With new management in senior positions at a time when I was recovering from my heart problem and attempting to control the company's incredible growth, what followed was, later on, easy to understand. There was a lack of proper reporting systems, a lack of proper supervision by me, and a new executive team that was doing what they thought was right to continue to build the company. It wasn't "lean and mean" the way we would have done it and in the meantime we didn't give them a system that was easy to grow with.

In a short time, through a combination of building up excess inventory and drawing down more bank debt by people who didn't quite know what they were doing, unforeseen and hidden problems began to emerge. The new team at the top saw that there were problems but chose to sweep them under the rug.

I didn't think my health issue was impacting the company at the time, but it obviously interfered with my ability to pay attention to all the details. I didn't realize how big the problems were under the surface. Had my health been better, I would not have delegated as much as I did and I believe I would have seen the underlying problems more closely.

I had returned to Marchon in June and we had scheduled some meetings that summer to review first half results. And frankly, they didn't make sense.

To further complicate matters, we were in the process of installing an SAP computer system which gave us global capabilities. But the system was extremely complicated, which impeded the ability of our team to manage effectively. Jeff was no longer there at that point, and perhaps there was less than good implementation. Also, we were running the SAP system and our old system simultaneously, and the end result—and there's really no other way to put it—were numbers that just didn't add up.

For me, the biggest indication of a problem was that the company's gross margin had seen a dramatic decline. Where it was typically in the 65%-70% range, it was now in the high 50%'s.

At the summer meeting, I took the COO and CFO aside and said, "Gentlemen, we've got to be clear here. Gross margin is not revolutionary, it's evolutionary. It can't change. You've got to go back and check all your numbers because they can't be right."

They checked their numbers and it turned out they were correct.

We had several lines of credit with our banks that probably totaled

$100 million, but we had hardly ever touched these reserves. By the time we understood the problem, which was largely the company being over-inventoried and experiencing some stress due to our overseas initiatives, we were facing a huge dilemma. To try to stabilize the ship, our management team had tapped into our reserves over a period of several quarters to such an extent that those reserves were no longer available to us.

Clearly, decisions had been made to try to resolve the problems but, as I said, to also hide them, to the extent that when we became aware of them they could no longer be hidden. It was obvious that our management didn't understand the seriousness of the situation.

It was, indeed, a perfect storm: my health had sidelined me for a period to some degree, and compelled us to delegate to managers who committed some critical errors, at a time when there was pressure on our cash flow due to excess inventory and the funding of our growth.

As I dug into the problems, I realized that it was like peeling back the layers of an onion only to find still more layers.

By October, it was clear that we were in serious trouble, a disquieting feeling when you're running a company that had never had a problem before. I took back control of the company (I actually didn't think I had lost control), and focused on the problems at hand. I didn't know how hard it would be to fix them.

On October 15, we sent an urgent message out to all the country managers around the world, advising that all decisions for the time being were going to come out of New York, and that all further expansion plans were to be put on hold while we reviewed operations. We didn't tell them about the problems.

It was absolutely imperative that we keep the events that had befallen Marchon under wraps, because the situation dictated that you not tell everybody everything. There was too much at stake: we didn't want the customers alarmed, or the sales people, or our vendors, or the internal team. And we certainly didn't want our competitors to find out.

But while, on the one hand, we remained silent on the company's problems, on the other we had to deal with them. Just by reasserting our roles in reviewing all decisions allowed us to continue to manage global expansion.

I was responsible for everything; my view was that I got the company in trouble and I had to be the one to get it out.

This is where my partners were really great. We all recognized the problems, and they could have easily shot me in the head because I was in charge. But instead of getting angry at me (which I would have probably done had I been them) they were both extremely supportive. They basically said, "Al, do what you've got to do to fix it and we're here to support you."

It was probably an event that could have ripped the company apart. But my partners recognized that if it was going to be fixed it would have to be me to fix it.

When I began, I was of the belief that it would take me about ninety days to clean up Dodge City, so to speak. It took me two-and-a-half years.

I underestimated the amount of time it would take because I didn't realize how dramatically the company had grown. Imagine the company as an amoeba, growing and expanding in all directions in a very short period of time. Marchon had become this humongous organization operated by an over-abundance of people all brought on board to help manage its incredible growth, and having to do it manually because the systems that were in place were simply not helpful.

It had to be fixable; there was no other option. If it wasn't fixable, the company was dead. Marchon was our baby, and we couldn't let our baby die.

We, as partners, had built the company brick by brick. We knew it well; its basic strengths and weaknesses, and we knew our industry well. The shift in management, of running the company on a day-to-day basis, had only happened within the last couple of years. We knew what we needed to do, and that was to make some tough decisions.

We had to analyze the company quickly, determine what was working and what was not working. We had to stop and fix what wasn't working while what was working continued to grow. And this process had to take place on a global basis.

It really just took the right guy at the right time and place, and—in all modesty—that was me. Had a third-party consultant, an outsider, come in to drive a turnaround he wouldn't know what to do and would probably just take his best shot. As an insider, I knew how to surgically attack the problem, fix what had to be fixed.

There was a tremendous number of things to be done, and they needed to be done by a surgeon who knew his patient and had the authority and vision to do it. It might have been a daunting task for an outsider, but a lot less daunting for me.

We had a great group of people, but clearly too many of them and some were expendable. We wound up reducing our workforce world-wide by something in the range of 20%-25%.

And all this had to be done as surreptitiously as possible, a tough thing to do when you terminate a large number of employees who will be out in the marketplace looking for jobs. I can't emphasize enough how dangerous the whole situation was. We needed our customers to remain loyal and our sales reps to keep the faith. We needed to keep our competition from eating us alive. We would have faced these scenarios had word gotten out.

We had to restructure our pricing policy, dump under-performing products, and actually rebuild a lot of the company. At that time and for about two years after that, I was working seven days a week. I'd get maybe two hours or so of sleep a night. It was nerve-racking. I remember saying to my wife, Gayle, that the situation is either going to kill me or I'm going to turn my army around.

Our vendor relationships became especially important to us at that time. We went to our vendors, especially our few big ones, sat down with them and told them we needed some help with dating terms. They all said "no problem". Considering how much of a bind we were in, just receiving an additional thirty to sixty days payment terms (something we had never done previously) created, maybe, an additional $50 million in cash flow.

The banks were pretty unhappy with us, as they should have been.

Our results had always gone one way and now, out of the blue, they turned. Our credit line, which up until then we only used sparingly, had been significantly drawn down.

They brought in a company to evaluate our assets and push us to shed anything that wasn't core. All they came up with was our West Coast computer company, OfficeMate, a little investment we hadn't paid much attention to. We were told to dump it.

"Dump it? What do you think we're going to get for it?"

"A million," they replied.

We then impressed upon them that we were facing a $50 million problem and a million bucks wasn't going to do much to remedy it.

Ultimately, we overruled them and didn't sell it. And in retrospect, I'm very glad we didn't because this single asset was instrumental in our negotiations to sell our company later on. We saw potential in keeping it, but not even we saw the potential value in it.

During the recovery process toward the end of 2004, it became imperative that we raise more cash and as the banks were no longer going to be lending to us, we looked to outside investors.

We interviewed a number of them and contrary to the way we thought they would be, they came on like a pack of wolves salivating over red meat. Initially, they didn't want equity in the deal but that changed as our talks proceeded.

Then, in December, we met with Lynn Tilton, a New York financier who had recently started her own investment firm, Patriarch Partners LLC, which specialized in funding (and sometimes acquiring) distressed businesses. Tilton was a graduate of Yale and Columbia and did tours of duty at Morgan Stanley, Goldman Sachs and Merrill Lynch. She was, to say the least, colorful (years later, she was pursued by the Securities and Exchange Commission for alleged fraud).

She hit it off with me and she liked our story. She agreed to provide us with a substantial loan with some key caveats. She would not ask for equity, but we had to agree to a hefty interest rate and a significant penalty rate for prepayment. Also, we had shared our 2005 forecasts with Lynn and were told that if we stumbled and missed our covenants, or didn't make our sales numbers for the first quarter, Marchon would be hers.

We entered 2005 with a great deal of optimism. We believed that our army was solid, the image and reputation of the company remained solid, the company restructure and the new product arsenal were solid, and we were expecting magic to happen.

We rolled the dice because we believed in our company. But when January sales didn't materialize the way we forecast we began to panic. When February followed suit we were sweating big time. What the hell was going on? It was like we were out of control; I really thought we had good forecasts. I remember discussing the situation with our attorneys, asking them what would happen if we didn't make it, knowing full well what the answer was. "You'll be done," they said.

And then March came and we hit it out of the park. I remember it as a "Thank God" moment. I couldn't figure out why it hadn't happened like that in January and February. But after that we started making the numbers consistently. And very quickly, there it was. Marchon went from being a wonderful company to a disaster to a wonderful company again.

We came out of it beautifully. In fact, we came out of it so beautifully that we actually exceeded our expectations. You have to do a lot of great things to turn the company and hit your goals for gross margin, EBITDA and net profit to return them to their levels prior to the problem. We overshot any goals we could have ever imagined.

After two-plus grueling years, I was gratified to see that the good and challenging job I had done saving the company paid off with financial numbers that went through the roof.

By 2007, we had a tremendously efficient, beautifully operating company. The SAP computer system was still a problem. But because we had implemented so many positive operational changes, even that was manageable.

When all the corporate chaos was completely and finally behind us, we and Marchon were four years older. We were beginning to mentally prepare for the company's Twenty-Fifth Anniversary in 2008, certain to be a big and very welcome event.

But the optical industry continued to change and change rapidly. It started to turn from an entrepreneurial, family-run industry operating under tight controls to corporate and global. Under those circumstances a company could implode (as did the German eyewear firm, Optyl) or it could dramatically succeed, like Luxottica. Regardless it's very hard to go from the highly managed family-run model to worldwide corporate with its many variables that you cannot control.

I looked at Luxottica and I saw that they dominated Italy, but they were able to develop systems for the rest of Europe, dependent on a personal culture that allowed for the many differences from country to country. Del Vecchio was better prepared for global expansion than we were. We were still a very American company ensconced in American culture. Those realizations made me reflect on the future.

In order for Marchon to survive and thrive going forward it would have to explore new directions, which meant that there was likely still more change to come.

CHAPTER 10

THE BIG DEAL

WITH MARCHON SOLIDLY back on course, and with profitability and cash flow restored, (and our obligations to Lynn Tilton satisfied) we were ready for the next stage in the company's development.

The optical market continued to change at an incredible pace; the big were getting bigger and there was consolidation on all sides. Retail was undergoing major changes as buying groups and doctor alliances became more powerful, and new concepts like online optical retailing emerged and threatened to be extremely disruptive. Luxottica was king, or should I say still king (they went on to buy sunglass giant Oakley, a $600 million company, in November of 2007 for $2.1 billion). We had some big decisions to make.

By 2006, we were compelled to evaluate our options. Ours was the third largest eyewear company in the world, and the only privately-held American company of that stature. We had, I'd say, nearly 2,500 employees effectively operating in one-hundred countries, 30,000 U.S. customers (another 10,000 served by OfficeMate) and roughly a half-billion in sales. But our two top competitors were highly diversified, comfortable in their global strategies and generally outpacing the rest of the industry, including us. We were the biggest fish in a smaller pond.

Could Marchon remain a stand-alone company? A succession plan wasn't in the cards because we had established a rule early on that no offspring of the owners could ever work at Marchon. Hence, we saw three options ahead: go public, align with another complementary company, or do nothing.

Doing nothing was not really an option, and we had entertained the idea of taking the company public on several occasions but always rejected it. Finding that compatible partner seemed to be the way to go, and the best choice for the company's future.

We identified six companies that we thought could be great partners, and over a period of six months, I met with all six casually, contacting the senior executive of each. The global investment firm, the Blackstone Group, was assigned to put together a prospectus on the company. We were looking for an economic tie—either with a partner or a purchaser.

It was determined that all candidates had to be strategic buyers because it was important to us that Marchon—its worldwide staff and sales teams—remain intact; a financial buyer would very possibly dismantle the company or eliminate parts of it to increase its value to the next buyer. We didn't want to see that kind of disruption happen to our people. So the logical prospect would be someone who owned a frame company or someone in optical who wanted to own a frame company and was big enough and financially capable of putting the deal together.

After reviewing the six companies, I determined that there were three that had serious interest, and were of interest to Marchon. (Luxottica was on the list and had expressed interest in purchasing us, but we felt strongly that if that took place our 2,500 employees around the world would find their jobs in jeopardy, many of our operations would be shut down and Del Vecchio would absorb the business without missing a beat, reducing costs by possibly $100 million to $200 million in the process.)

Of the three contenders, the one which impressed us the most was VSP Vision Care (formerly known as Vision Service Plan), the leading managed vision care provider in the country. They had a provider panel of over 25,000 optometrists, serving some 55 million consumers nationwide and more than half of all Fortune 500 companies. And they were extremely well-capitalized.

We knew next to zero about managed vision care, but we did know that Luxottica had a very large presence in that market segment through its own managed care company, EyeMed. While second to VSP in terms of covered lives and revenue, it nonetheless gave Luxottica a decided comparative advantage, especially as they had a ready-made network of providers through Lenscrafters, Pearle, and other retail businesses they acquired. Effectively, they were operating EyeMed as a loss leader to increase their eyewear sales and not like an insurer.

Through a potential union with VSP, we could realize the ability to create a group that might very effectively compete with Lux, which was our constant battle. We also felt, after some study, that managed care would be the driver for the independent segment of the industry in the years ahead, basically helping to make eyewear more affordable and building patient traffic.

It turned out that Rob Lynch, the recently installed president and CEO of VSP, understood this dynamic well and had as much interest in Marchon as we had in his company. (Ironically, in July of 2006, Rob had contacted Oakley to determine their interest in getting together only to learn that they were already "far down the road" with another buyer. When, a month later, Rob discovered that the buyer was Luxottica, and that they would readily pay $2.1 billion for a $600 million company, he admitted that that was a road VSP would not choose to take.)

Although he had been on the VSP board for nine years, Rob was quite new to the industry from a day-to-day operational standpoint. He quickly understood that the average VSP provider was deriving 40% of his revenues from eye exams and professional services and 60% from materials. It didn't take him long to also conclude that as Essilor and Luxottica amassed more and more market share and continued to expand their product portfolios through continuous acquisition, it was only a matter of time before these behemoths were dictating pricing terms to VSP, among others.

Rob told us he had gotten nervous about the VSP supply chain going forward, about losing control of their pricing mechanisms, and surmised that in order for his company to remain competitive it had to get bigger and become more relevant on the materials side of the business.

They had a presence in the lens and lab businesses and also owned a small frame company. Rob believed they needed to acquire a major frame company to maintain their competitive position.

So it turned out that we were on each other's dance cards. Now we just had to connect. Rob didn't know us, nor for that matter any other frame suppliers on a personal basis. So he turned to a VSP exec that knew the frame business and knew Marchon. But he never called.

In frustration, Rob turned to Steve Baker, the president of VSP's web portal Eyefinity, who knew Jim McGrann, our CIO. Through those two we managed to arrange a meeting with Rob at the American Optometric Association Convention at Boston in late June, 2007.

Rob was a very affable and a very smart guy. He knew that VSP had to make a big move in order to remain competitive and relevant. That first meeting went on for three-and-a-half hours. We talked about everything, and found, somewhat surprisingly, that we agreed on most issues, particularly the future of the optical industry.

But the compatibility didn't end there: we were both primarily dedicated to the independent eyecare professional; we both had global ambitions; and we both had made a commitment to having an important digital presence—Marchon via OfficeMate, and VSP via Eyefinity.

That one asset of ours really impressed Rob and showed him the further benefits of a marriage. OfficeMate was a desktop practice management solution. Eyefinity was a claims processing web portal. The synergy between the two was obvious. Rob viewed OfficeMate as a strong complement to their current digital business, and the cherry on top of the Marchon sundae.

We also came to like each other a lot, which helped smooth the way for bringing the deal together. I liked what VSP was doing with their business; it made sense to me to use managed care as a vehicle to drive patients into independent practices which would certainly play to our advantage, and represented about 80% of our customer base.

Marchon, in turn, had a longstanding reputation as more than just a frame supplier. We had brought practice education on marketing and merchandising to a new level. Between the two companies we could easily provide a wealth of services and products that embraced one critical purpose—to make eye care professionals the best they could be in both the medical and retail aspects of their businesses.

VSP also had a for-profit frames company called Altair that was generating about $50 million per year. They had a business model that really intrigued me: an exclusive telesales team offering customers product on a consignment basis—very different from the Marchon model. They also had some attractive licenses like Tommy Bahama and Joseph Abboud, and we knew that, given the chance, we could assist them in getting more—especially if they were more suited to Altair's price point and portfolio than Marchon's.

I felt we were in a great position to help VSP in a number of ways, while creating with them this new hybrid which was better positioned than either company individually to compete in the future optical world. Also, VSP traditionally was always looking within; with the inclusion of Marchon they would begin looking without. We felt, too, that we could bring them closer to their providers, our customers.

One specific item that was a high priority for Rob Lynch was the international expansion of VSP. Apparently, in visiting with a number of their large, multinational customers, Rob learned of their desire to be able to provide VSP services to employees in other global markets. "Why not Canada or the U.K.?" several of them asked him.

Of course, Marchon already had an extensive international network and infrastructure, so it would be easy for us to open those doors for VSP, and introduce them to the key players and decision makers in the markets they were targeting.

But despite all the commonalities and shared ambitions, the two companies were culturally different. VSP was a West Coast company, espousing a collaborative, corporate culture; Marchon was an East Coast company and a classic entrepreneurship, with me and Larry as the key decision makers. VSP was institutional and significantly regulated; Marchon was anything but. Finally, VSP was set up as a community benefits-based not for profit, meaning it has no owners; Marchon was very much a "for profit" business and it was readily clear who the ownership was.

Also, in my view, VSP had a little too much fat and Marchon was run lean and skinny. Rob Lynch, on the other hand, believed we needed more organizational depth. He pointed out to me that I had nineteen people as direct reports, and no succession plan, meaning that if something happened to me it would take the management group a while to learn to make decisions the way I did—a valid point. I had to agree, finally, that I was doing too much, which prevented me from dedicating energy to scaling our business.

VSP would be committed to Marchon's growth and autonomy. Hence, it was apparent to both of us that we each were highly motivated to orchestrate a marriage, and we made the decision right after that initial meeting to begin negotiating in earnest. By July we were in the thick of it.

The due diligence process was arduous, and seemingly took much longer than I would have anticipated. Of course, as a privately-held company Marchon was subjected to considerable scrutiny. The VSP due diligence team looked in every closet and under every carpet. Certainly, they needed to make sure that our numbers—our sales, gross profit and EBITDA—supported our claims, and that our international network was set up on a sound legal footing, a country-by-country investigative effort.

They also wanted to be assured that our brands would remain on board. So during this period, we visited with each of our licensors and advised them of what we were planning. Their enthusiasm for the merger was universal. They needed strong licensees, and while they were all happy with Marchon as it was, they also realized that a stronger Marchon was better for them.

At the same time, we were also trying to figure out what this new animal would look like on the back end. Here, we agreed on a number of things: each company would remain in its respective headquarters and the two staffs would pretty much remain intact. We'd run our business and they'd run theirs, albeit with some shared resources and people.

Also, Larry and I would commit to remaining in our positions for at least four years and then entertain the idea of consulting relationships. Candidly, I never just wanted to sell and walk away, nor did Larry. It was important to me for the sake of our people to make sure that everything continued smoothly.

Rob was also fairly emphatic about our staying on. He noted that in his previous roles managing acquisitions, the ones that didn't work were the ones in which the key people weren't retained. We appreciated his point of view and certainly wanted to make it a seamless transition.

The process continued to move along…slowly. As a highly regulated business, VSP had to obtain approval for the deal from regulators in California and Connecticut. Regulators turned out to be a big hurdle. Also, they continued to conduct a very intensive, precise fact-finding mission with their due diligence

Negotiations shuffled along into 2008, Marchon's Twenty-Fifth Anniversary year. We were going to celebrate it in a number of ways at the Vision Expo trade shows. Also, *Women's Wear Daily*, the world's leading fashion newspaper, and *Vision Monday*, a prominent optical industry trade magazine, each produced extensive, multi-page editorial sections on the growth, accomplishments and innovations of Marchon over our two-and-a-half decades.

We did a lot of great stuff for the Twenty-Fifth Anniversary: we honored our top 2,500 U.S. accounts with a commemorative plaque which commended them for providing their patients with superior Marchon products and customer service, and a "thank you" book (which actually told you how to write thank you notes), and our branches overseas did much the same thing. We had a special Twenty-Fifth Anniversary logo developed, and starting in the first quarter of 2008, we had produced custom edition bags of M&Ms thanking accounts for their business, which we stuffed into every frame shipment. The Twenty-Fifth

Anniversary logo appeared everywhere—invoices, websites, letterhead, you name it.

And for the sales crew, we took everyone to an all-inclusive resort in Cancun, Mexico for our annual sales meeting.

We wanted to make sure this anniversary was memorable and I'm glad to say that we succeeded.

In the meantime, word was getting around that VSP was on the verge of buying "a big frame company," and industry people—including our own—were speculating about who it would be. This had us nervous as we didn't want word to leak out beforehand. We believed it would impact our people, our customers and our business somewhat negatively and provide selling points to our competitors.

Our impatience began to control our demeanor to some extent. Rob and I had occasional, and sometimes heated, arguments about myriad things, such as what was real entrepreneurship. (Rob made a case for the fact that VSP had developed a number of "start up" businesses, like Altair, Eyefinity and their laboratory network in an entrepreneurial way, and I countered by reminding him that Marchon started literally from scratch without the benefit of a large corporate parent to nurture it.)

On another occasion, we got into a shouting match over a cultural difference regarding their email addressing system. They used first names @ VSP.com. I was incredulous. Marchon's system was first initial followed by last name, sidestepping any confusion. "You're a big organization," I said, "How many Johns do you have, how many Jims? How will someone tell one from the other?"

These kinds of confrontations seemed trivial, but I think they pointed to my overall frustration and my occasional, vague doubts about the deal going through.

We finally hammered out a blueprint for the new VSP Vision Care. There would be four operating units: the VSP insurance business which would be headed by Gary Brooks as president; the ophthalmic services and laboratory unit which included VSP-owned labs and partner labs, in addition to VSP's three-hundred contract labs, to be run by

Don Oakley; the eyewear division, led by Marchon and me with Altair and its president, Steve Wright, reporting to me; and a "business solutions" division, encompassing OfficeMate and Eyefinity, to be run by Jim McGrann. By design, the two companies would "cross-pollinate" with their respective people and ideas.

Marchon was also 50% owner of the small custom retail interiors business called Eye Designs which VSP, always looking for a greater breadth of service to offer their doctors, agreed to purchase. Additionally, there was our relationship with the web portal, VisionWeb which we maintained with Essilor, Luxottica and a few other companies. Despite the fact that it was competitive with Eyefinity, Rob believed that it was a benefit to the industry and would contribute to making optical transactions much easier to execute.

Despite all the preparation and planning, there was still no deal in the offing. For Marchon, it was "business as usual" and we were on our way to a $600 million year, with our five key brands each producing $100 million in sales, complemented by an assortment of smaller brands collectively generating the additional $100 million. And still the rumors persisted about a big VSP acquisition, and they were getting closer to home.

Eventually, I would become very involved with VSP. Although I wasn't a member of the board, I attended most of their meetings. The board was very committed to expanding VSP's materials business and developing a global strategy.

I really enjoyed the VSP marketing people, but a number of them found me "challenging," which I took as a euphemism for "intimidating." As a collegial, collaborative group, they weren't used to a single manager like me who had a very distinct view on just about everything (and yes, I could get into the weeds sometimes). I knew how my style resonated with people, but I also knew it was highly effective. I'd have to admit that, at that point, the VSP culture was starting to change my perspective a bit.

I felt I was good for the overall business and was very dedicated to helping Rob Lynch shape the strategy for this new entity. I believe I really impressed Rob, so much so that VSP created an Al Berg "MBA course," based on my management philosophy, which I delivered at several locations, including the company's Sacramento headquarters. I always packed the house.

By mid-summer of 2008, having done this dance with VSP for twelve months, we needed to bring the deal to its resolution or move on. Larry and I made our feelings known to the VSP brass (as if this was the first they were hearing of it) and they told us they were ready to proceed.

On Friday, August 15, 2008, the deal was finally done. The payment was $735 million in cash, the result was a $3.3 billion company, and by the following Monday we were ready to officially announce it to the world.

The market's reaction was very largely positive. We got a little pushback from doctors who were Marchon customers but not VSP providers and expressed concern that the merger would somehow change their relationship with us. Some of our OfficeMate docs, too, were worried about VSP obtaining their data. And there were several industry "gadflies"—or consultants—who felt that it was to their advantage to stir the pot of doubt they were brewing in order to keep their eye doctor clients in the fold.

All these concerns were minor and quickly faded away. Many industry people realized that the move would mean a stronger Marchon and a stronger VSP, and a much more potent alternative to Luxottica.

After the announcement, our friend Leonardo Del Vecchio took the gloves off, so to speak. For decades, Luxottica had maintained a position that Marchon, while still a competitor, was to be largely left untouched in deference to Del Vecchio's close relationship with Ruth and Frank White.

But once the ownership changed, Marchon became fair game. Lux aggressively pursued our licenses, Coach and Michael Kors, and ultimately got them.

In the meantime, it was very important to us that Marchon's worldwide team learn all the true details of the deal (as opposed to the many wild rumors they were receiving), and appreciate their value to the company going forward. We had told the sales staff the weekend before we closed and we prepared to hold "town hall" meetings with all other employees. All our managers got together and determined how the announcement would be presented; we didn't want anything left to improvisation.

And as I mentioned prior, every Marchon employee received a bonus based on the length of their tenure with the company, a $50 million tab. We felt it was important to share in Marchon's success with the people who helped to make it happen.

We also felt that in order to accommodate a smooth transition, we would recruit a new company CEO who would have several years with me and Larry before our next chapter in the story. Claudio Gottardi had been the CEO of Italian eyewear company, Safilo USA, for a number of years after holding several executive positions with the Padua-based parent. He was now a free agent, and we thought he'd make a great candidate as he had extensive experience managing a large frame company. With VSP's approval he came on board.

The proceeds from the sale were largely divided by Larry and me. Jeff's 20% share was divided among his siblings and their children.

One odyssey was coming to an end, and another just beginning. I felt confident that we had actually planted the seeds to grow a great new company that was better equipped to compete in the optical world now and in the future.

We began to prepare for what was to come with Claudio at the helm. There were still trade shows to attend, sales to be made, new eyewear products to create. Unknown to us and most everyone else in the United States at the time, the economy had begun to falter in December of the previous year. Suddenly, housing values plummeted, mortgage holders defaulted, and financial giants tumbled.

Ironically, one month to the day after we concluded the VSP deal, Lehman Brothers, a venerated, old securities firm based in midtown Manhattan, declared bankruptcy. Other financial institutions followed. Soon there was talk of huge government bailouts. Even the auto industry was heavily impacted, with General Motors on the verge of collapsing. And of course, the stock market experienced a major meltdown.

Larry and I counted our blessings. We knew that if the deal had been delayed a month the results would have been disastrous with the sale price deflating rapidly. Fortunately too, the transaction was brand new and we were unable to make any investments at a time when the stock market was about to hit rock bottom. By the time we were ready to put our money to work, the market was so depressed that many blue chip stocks became real bargains and our financial portfolios over a relatively short period of time came into full bloom.

Over the years, Marchon has had to contend with naysayers. We heard every lame rationalization for our success: right place at the right time, Marcolin propped them up, and the one I really love to hear… they were just lucky.

To be honest, I feel I am blessed with luck. I have a great family, a great business and a great life. But I also know that luck is earned. And as such, there's a quote that's dubiously attributed to Thomas Jefferson:"I am a great believer in luck, and I find the harder I work the more I have of it."

LAST WORD:
MAKING A DIFFERENCE

WHEN WE SET out to create what would become Marchon, we didn't think we were reinventing the wheel (or reinventing eyewear, for that matter). We didn't have to be the first; we just had to be the best. Eighty percent of success is just doing it better. The other 20% is innovation, consistency, reliability.

Our objective was to build one of the greatest companies in the industry. Unlike a number of our domestic competitors, we weren't in business simply to make a sale today—we were focused on tomorrow's sale.

Actually, so long as they believed they were just selling frames and not building a business, they weren't really competitors.

From the first day we opened our doors we were looking five years down the road. Then ten years. We gathered our resources and created a mechanism to accommodate a company servicing 20,000 customers when we only had 10,000. We didn't maximize profitability by having excess capacity. We viewed it as an asset and the only time it was a liability was if we didn't eventually need it.

But every time we went through the exercise of weighing the pros and the cons, the answer always came back: build it! Some might call that reckless, but we felt those were valid business decisions. If you don't build it, you can't grow with it and it becomes a self-fulfilling failure. We had a vision for the business based on that firm belief and everything we did was in pursuit of that vision.

Among the most important factors in creating a successful eyewear business was our backgrounds. We had the Avant Garde (eventually Luxottica) playbook. It taught us the basics of building a company poised for the future industry, in contrast to many of the U.S. players whose companies were rooted in methodologies and presumptions of the past. Many of them were smart entrepreneurs who were looking for security as opposed to taking risks. From our perspective we weren't taking risks—they're only risks if you're wrong. You cannot build a big company without that instinct.

Also, two of us—Jeff and Larry—essentially grew up in the industry. I, the third partner, was an outsider who had come to the industry without a lot of baggage and I believe that gave me an advantage. All I knew about optical came from my brief experience at Avant Garde, and at the outset that was all I needed to know. The Avant Garde experience with the Whites, along with my Harvard training and the unique skills of my partners, provided the ingredients for a very special company.

But Marchon's true success was based on one single business practice: perfect execution. With perfect execution comes unsurpassed service for your customers and your sales team, and that was our key point of differentiation. It was also the foundation upon which Marchon's reputation as an outstanding service provider was built.

There were many companies selling eyewear in the early 1980s; some well, others less so. And where the lesser companies were usually weakest was in their execution.

There are possibly fifteen ingredients that make up perfect execution in the eyewear business, and every one of them is critical. That assumption powered our operating culture.

A lot of our competitors looked at us and asked themselves, "How can I duplicate this?" And they would discern some of the elements. They would take the low-hanging fruit, the obvious pieces, and copy them, but in the end not achieve the same result.

It's like having the recipe for the most spectacular chocolate cake that others would try to copy, but never truly be able to duplicate.

One of our most important ingredients in our particular recipe was our people, certainly our in-house team but more specifically our sales and customer service staffs. They were our touch-points with the customers. For many customers, they were Marchon.

It was imperative that our field and customer service people be great communicators, and not just sellers of eyewear. That was especially true for our field salespeople. As eyewear became more fashion-focused and more complex, as fashion designers came into the mix, it was vital that our sales people serve as trainers and educators, marketing consultants and store display experts. Again, this was the level of service that distinguished us in a very competitive field.

As a consequence, it was our philosophy to treat our sales and customer service people as our customers. If they came to us with an idea or a complaint from the field, we addressed it immediately. They were advocating for their customers and we fully understood that.

Most importantly, we valued and respected our people and awarded their unique talents. Sometimes we had to make hard decisions for the sake of the company. Our people may have been uncomfortable with a decision we made (such as instituting multiple sales forces), but they understood our logic.

As operators, we would sometimes argue, but our arguments weren't driven by ego or personal agendas. We were all subservient to the right decision, the right answer for the company, and everyone at Marchon knew it.

Over the years, as the optical industry became more complex and the dictates of the product called for a thorough understanding of European fashion and designer branding, the service needs of the eye care practitioner became greater and greater. They required fashion education and marketing training. They required responsive company representatives who knew what they wanted and needed.

As I've suggested before, that was Marchon's sweet spot. That's where we truly excelled. And until the sale of the company, that was a perch upon which Marchon sat exclusively. We knew our customers extremely well. We knew, for example, that the optometrist was fre-quently the business owner and needed education about running a better business. We knew the dispensers needed knowledge about the products themselves, the features and benefits as well as the brand sto-ries behind them. They needed to know how to present those products to the consumer.

Another important element of the Marchon success formula was our imperative to always look bigger than we were and invite our cus-tomers and sales people to see us as a significant supplier. This was especially true when the company was still young. As a new company, how do you break through the clutter? It's extremely important that the customer believes you're substantial and that they hear that same appraisal from others.

Everything we did was designed to reinforce our image and mes-sage. We had the vision to be one of the largest companies in the opti-cal industry and everything we did—from choosing to partner with Marcolin, to building the computer system, to grooming our internal staff and recruiting a great sales team—was done in pursuit of that vision.

Most importantly, we positioned ourselves against Avant Garde from the outset and that positioning was highly effective in reinforcing our image.

The industry was starting to expand and change very rapidly, but a lot of companies didn't change their models. Importers were starting to grow and domestic suppliers were starting to decline but didn't react to it. They could control distribution through wholesalers and try to block the importers, but didn't recognize that direct selling was a big part of the new model.

It's amazing when I think of where the optical industry was when we began and where it wound up when we sold twenty-five years lat-er: there was no proliferation of designer brands as there came to be; wholesalers were a significant distribution force, but direct sellers over-took them; U.S. product gave way to European product as Europe be-came the primary fashion supplier, but that changed again as the focus moved to Japan and then China, which emerged with higher-quality product; the single sales force model was replaced by multiple sales forces, a practice that had first become prevalent in Italy.

One significant trend that impacted just about everything was the rapid growth of managed vision care. While there are a plethora of different opinions about managed care, I believe it actually helped the industry's growth by making the product more cost-effective for the consumer. The benefit is inherently a discount, and more affordable product means more sales.

But of course, the watershed moment for the optical industry in those twenty-five years occurred in April, 1995 when it was suddenly announced that Luxottica had acquired U.S. Shoe, parent of the superstore chain Lenscrafters, for $1.4 billion, bringing them closer than anyone else to the ultimate customer.

From that point on, Luxottica just proceeded to barrel through the industry. Today, there's no one truly competing with Luxottica, as much as I'd like to believe that Marchon is there.

And now, with the merger of Essilor and Luxottica, that assumption is cast in stone. I, for one, believe that EssilorLuxottica will end up competing with about half the industry. The other half will be mostly niche players who may actually receive business opportunities as this new corporate entity becomes consumed with trying to digest all that's on its plate.

Think of it as some giant animal that occasionally shakes its massive body, casting off fleas for the smaller, hungry animals to devour.

I've spent a lot of my career focusing on the comings and goings of Luxottica. It was a motivator for me. Someone once asked me who my mentor was, and at first I didn't think I had one. Then it occurred to me who my mentor was: Leonardo Del Vecchio. As I mentioned, I really didn't know him personally but, hell, I lived with him for twenty-five years, and I watched his moves carefully. Del Vecchio can be ruthless, and he can be a gambler—two character traits that make him a very tough business opponent. He also knows that the greater the fashion, the greater the risk.

Much of the competitive landscape today is the result of something he or his company did that changed it.

For one thing, Luxottica spearheaded the global strategy. Today, there are a handful of players—Lux, Marchon, Safilo, Marcolin, DeRigo, Kering—that enjoy the benefits of a global footprint. They obtain the top designer brands, attract the most talented people and garner the most retailer and consumer recognition. They also have the most substantial financial resources.

Luxury brand giants Kering and LVMH are especially well poised to dominate the worldwide eyewear marketplace. Both control myriad powerhouse brands—Kering, for example, owns Gucci and Yves St. Laurent; LVMH has Christian Dior, Louis Vuitton and Givenchy. Both in recent years have staked out major positions within the eyewear industry. Kering did it from scratch, building an eyewear company from the ground up on the strength of the Gucci brand. LVMH did it differently (and to my way of thinking, better) by acquiring Marcolin, which of course already had the necessary structures in place.

As for our domestically-based compatriots, I think of many of them as "trapped" companies, meaning they didn't take the necessary steps to evolve as the industry evolved. As a consequence, it's anybody's guess where they will end up.

These companies also have to contend with an ever-changing customer base. What was once an industry of 35,000 independent "mom and pop" optical businesses is now dominated by practitioner alliances, buying groups and private equity players who are rolling up these practices into vast, multi-location chain entities. On top of that, there is now a substantial and growing online retail optical category. And I'm sure there are more changes still to come.

For my part, I look back on the nearly three decades of my career with enormous satisfaction. I loved what I did. I found an industry that was coming into its own, combining fashion with health care. The source of my success was in finding an industry with potential, and more importantly finding a product category that was evolving and had a future. A consumer product category—I wouldn't have enjoyed industrial products.

I was lucky. I happened upon a great industry that I loved, a product category that was perfect, and a great partnership that was critically important to the company's success. Not many people can say that.

Of course, I also worked hard. I put in many long days and spent many, many hours on airplanes and in hotels around the world. Sometimes I saw a lot of trees but not the forest.

Did this affect my family? Surely. But we accepted that as my necessary commitment to building a great company for all involved. I'm not sure we initially understood the impact and meaning of such a commitment, but I can say we were thrilled with the company that the team built.

There are many emblems of our success: the security that money gives you and provides for your family and those who come after; the ability to control your own destiny. I was very fortunate to achieve what I set out to achieve from the time I was a student at Harvard.

How would I like Marchon to be remembered? As a very exciting company that helped bring the optical industry into the 21st century and served as a good bridge with the past. Whether judged by product, marketing or systems, I believe ours was an excellent company to work for and buy from.

Did Marchon help to make the industry a little better? The answer is yes. It is very satisfying to know that for thousands of people—customers, employees, colleagues—Marchon was a great experience.

It emphatically was for me.

—Al Berg
Old Westbury, N.Y.

THE (BUSINESS) WORLD
ACCORDING TO AL

HAD HE NOT been a business executive, Al Berg would probably have been a great professor—a much sought after one. Al had a deep appreciation for learning and apparently believed that everything was a "teachable moment".

Al believed steadfastly in honesty, directness and flawless execution. For many of his employees and colleagues he provided (somewhat inadvertently) life and business lessons, which many of them codified. Deb Ingino,(who had created an "Al Lessons Book" for herself) put it this way, "Al was the greatest professional influence on my life from 1988 to 2011".

Herewith, a bit paraphrased, are some of Al's lessons.

—EG

No decision is a decision. Every action you take, or don't take, has consequences and you need to be aware of what they are.

Be careful not to create Frankenstein's monster. Consider the unintended consequences of your actions. Don't create something that will eventually come back to bite you.

Face problems head on. When a problem emerges, don't sweep it under the rug. Drill down and examine all the facts.

Beware of the "Maitre D" response. Be cautious of people who tell you what they think you want to hear. Diner: "How's the chicken here?" Maitre D: "Oh, it's wonderful!"

If hindsight is 20/20, what can foresight be? Envision a future where you want to go and develop a well-thought-out plan to get there.

Execute, or be executed. You can give a customer superlative service for fifty days in a row, but if you stumble on the fifty-first that's what he'll remember.

Garbage in creates garbage out. Bad information leads to bad decision making.

Never be afraid to take risks if you have sufficiently thought things through. A risky decision made without proper analysis beforehand is reckless.

If you can't push the big rock up the hill, break it into little pieces. If a problem seems insurmountable, reduce it to its manageable components.

Think the way your competitor thinks and be fair in all dealings. Understanding your competitor's motivations, actions and biases is paramount to success. And finding the "sweet spot" in a business negotiation is a win-win for all involved.

IN REMEMBRANCE OF ALFRED KIT BERG

AL BERG WAS an incomparable, talented entrepreneur and a unique, larger-than-life human being. He loved his family, his business and his employees. He also loved truth and honesty, directness and sound knowledge. He was among a rare breed.

Those who worked for him all had virtually the same assessment of him as a boss: tough, challenging and fair. And there wasn't a single employee who didn't seek Al's approval and recognition.

The memorial service for Al was an emotional celebration of his life, attended by hundreds of his closest friends. The room was full to overflowing, making necessary a second room with a TV monitor to view the proceedings.

With eloquence and poise, family, friends and business associates eulogized Al. What they said and wrote was memorable and profoundly heartfelt. Here are some excerpts from the eulogies and written remembrances given by his wife, Gayle, and children, Jarret and Carly.

—*F.G.*

Al was someone who put his money where his mouth was. He wasn't afraid to speak up and say what he really thought and he'd lead by example. He knew the power that those who have money wield but he never did so without his very large heart. I believe that's what differentiated him from mostly everybody else—his kindness and generosity. He truly had a heart of gold!!! He was a mensch among men—and everybody knew it. You could count on him to be supportive of the countless good things that arise in the course of living life. He was the Lone Ranger in the fantasy of his mind but also found various ways to create and live out a variety of real episodes in his own life. Ultimately, he left the world a better place because of it.

—Gayle Berg

Dad was a man of action, and though I never was formally an employee of Al Berg, Inc., I'm not sure he ever knew. He was extremely driven and generous with his time. If you had his ear, he would analyze and problem-solve the thorniest of issues on the yellow legal pad. He'd scramble the chessboard on your behalf and then challenge you to solve. He would take your ideas and torch them in the crucible of his mind. Every twist and turn he would strategize like the chess master he was. Once resolved, his challenge was a directive to go out and DO. And do it well, and not to merely continue talking or complaining about cards dealt in an unfair world.

—Jarret Berg

August 2008 we were called to a family dinner. This was the night he was preparing to tell us he was officially selling Marchon and how proud he was. And as we are preparing to cook this lobster feast as a family, the power goes out. The irony is that one of the most exciting moments in my dad's life, where he could finally brag to us about his life's work, he was humbly brought back down to earth.

We had to cook lobsters using Sterno lamps and ate by candlelight that night. He turned it into a lesson of course about never getting too cocky or overly confident. It reminded us that in one moment, everything can be stripped away, and to never take anything for granted.

—*Carly Berg*